# BASIC DISCIPLESHIP LESSONS
## ADDITIONAL RESOURCES
### for
### New Life in Christ
### Keys to an Abundant Christian Life

I0087055

## CHURCH OF THE NAZARENE

### MESOAMERICA REGION

From Conversion to Baptism to Membership

•Discipleship•
abcde

Level B1 - From Conversion to Baptism
Youth and Adults

Level B2 – From Baptism to Membership
Youth and Adults

# Basic Discipleship Lessons-Additional Resources

Book of the series "Discipleship ABCDE"
Level B1 and B2 - From Conversion to Baptism to Membership

General Editor: Dr Mónica Mastronardi de Fernández
Material produced by: Discipleship Ministries, Church of the Nazarene Mesoamerica Region
www.SdmiResources.MesoamericaRegion.org

ISBN:978-1-63580-095-1

Quotes from the Scriptures are taken from the New International Version of the Bible

Design by: Juan Manuel Fernández

Translated from Spanish to English by:
Dr. Dorothy Bullón:
    Dictionary for New Believers
    History and Ministry of the Church of the Nazarene in the World
    God, The Owner of All Things
    How Should a Spirit-Filled Christian Live?
    Loving Like Jesus Did
Yadira Morales:
    Sharing Christ with My Family and Friends
    Discovering Jesus Every Day
Blanca Huertas:
    How to Read the Bible and Learn From It
    4 Steps to Becoming a Happy Tither
Lily González:
    United in the Family of God
    Receive Power
Monte Cyr:
    What Nazarenes Believe

Edited by: Monte Cyr

Printed in the United States

# Table of Contents

**What is Discipleship ABCDE?** ...............................................4

**Presentation** ...........................................................................6

**Additional Resources for NEW LIFE IN CHRIST**
*Level B1 - From Conversion to Baptism*

*United in the Family of God*...................................................7
  David González Pérez

*Discovering Jesus Every Day*...............................................17
  31 devotionals for new Christians in the Gospel of Luke
  Christian D. Sarmiento & Mónica E. Mastronardi de Fernández

*How to Read the Bible and Learn From It*...............................33
  Mónica E. Mastronardi de Fernández

*Dictionary for New Believers* ...............................................45
  Mónica E. Mastronardi de Fernández

**Additional Resources for KEYS TO AN ABUNDANT CHRISTIAN LIFE**
*Level B2 – From Baptism to Membership*

*What We Believe as Nazarenes* ............................................67
  Mónica E. Mastronardi de Fernández

*Loving Like Jesus Did* ..........................................................93
  C. Helmer Juárez

*History and Ministry of the Church of the
Nazarene in the World* ........................................................111
  Ruthie Córdova Carvallo

*How Should a Spirit-Filled Christian Live?* ..........................122
  Ulises Daniel Solís

*Sharing Christ With My Family and Friends* ......................... 130
  Juan Manuel Fernández

*God, The Owner of All Things* ........................................... 140
  Mónica Mastronardi de Fernández, Rubén E. Fernández

*You Will Receive Power* ..................................................... 154
  Stephen Manley

*4 Steps to Becoming a Happy Tither* .................................. 168
  Christian Sarmiento

# What is Discipleship ABCDE?

Making Christlike disciples in the nations is the foundation of the missionary work of the Church, and the main responsibility of its leadership (Ephesians 4:7-16). The work of discipleship is continuous and dynamic, that is, the disciple never stops growing in the Likeness of his Lord. This growth process, when it is healthy, occurs in all dimensions: as individuals (spiritual growth), in the corporate dimension (becoming part of the congregation of the church), in holiness of life (progressively becoming more like Jesus Christ), as well as in a life invested in service to God and others.

The ABCDE Discipleship Plan has been designed to contribute to the comprehensive formation of members of the churches of the Nazarene in the Mesoamerica Region. We have published materials to cover all discipleship levels.

This book corresponds to LEVEL B of discipleship, the second stage of the plan that begins when the person who has accepted Jesus Christ as Savior and Lord. LEVEL B has the purpose of guiding the new disciple and his discipler in the study of the biblical basis of the Christian life.

The level is developed in 2 books (or 1 packet of lessons entitled Basic Discipleship Lessons): New Life in Christ (B1) that focuses on preparation for baptism, and Keys to the Abundant Christian Life (B2) that aims to prepare the new disciple for active membership in the local church. This book is a companion book to those 2 books or packet, providing additional resources to flesh out more fully the truths of those lessons.

Dr. Monica Mastronardi de Fernández
  General Editor Discipleship ABCDE
  Church of the Nazarene - Mesoamerica Region

# ·DISCIPLESHIP·
# abcde
## church of the nazarene

**Level A | Approach**

Evangelism.

**Level B | Baptism and Membership**

Discipleship for New Believers.

**Level C | Continued Growth**

"Full of the Spirit" Discipleship.

**Level D
Ministry Development**

School of Leadership.

**Level D
Professional Development**

Specialized Training at
Theological Institutions.

**Level E | Education for Life and Service**

Wholistic Growth in Christlikeness.

# Presentation

I am very excited to welcome you to the greatest adventure in life ... growing and living as a disciple of Jesus Christ. At this time, it is likely that you have taken the first big step in your Christian life, when you asked Jesus to forgive you and cleanse you from your sins. If so, Jesus Christ is now your personal savior and is present in you life. This first step is wonderful, but it is only the beginning. Jesus wants to do more than just save you from you sins and give you eternal life. He wants to lead you to live your life according to his purposes. He wants to teach you how to love others and to serve others as he did.

To achieve this, the first thing we need to do is to grow in our relationship with Him, to learn to love God with our whole being, and to follow His example in all our ways of living. This process is known as DISCIPLESHIP, and the person who participates in it is called a DISCIPLE. Every Christian is called to participate in discipleship, and to live as a disciple of Jesus, for their whole life.

This resource that you have in front of you, among other related materials, is designed to help you on this journey of becoming more and more like Christ. As you study this resource with your discipler / teacher, you will be able to apply the teachings of the Word of God to your life and learn to walk closer and closer to Jesus, and at the same time, grow in your relationships with the Lord and with other people. Our desire from Discipleship Ministries is that you will continue to grow and serve for the rest of your life as a disciple, and that later on, you too can become a discipler by guiding others to become disciples of Jesus.

God bless you.

Rev. Monte Cyr

Discipleship Ministries Coordinator, Mesoamerica Region

# United in the Family of God

David González Pérez

## Introduction

**God created the perfect universe**. We read in the book of Genesis that what God did was "very good." But in spite of being perfect, man considered that for him, it was not good enough, and he wanted to make his own world, his own society. And he achieved it. However, the consequences were not long in coming. Since then, there have been endless problems, illnesses, disputes, divisions, wars, pain and finally, death.

So, the world cries out for a better society, the hope of a better life. That has been God's purpose, even when man rejected it at the beginning. The redemptive purpose of God includes the creation of a new humanity, which accepts the original plan of living in communion with Him and accepting His lordship; a new society for which there is no separation between people due to racial differences, gender, social class, nationality or any other class.

Many will think that this is only a dream, but no, it is a reality that God makes possible through his Church.

That's right, the Church is the people of God, who through the sacrifice of Jesus on the cross can live in harmony with Him, who now has life and represents for humanity a light that gives hope of a new society.

## Welcome Home

When we accept Jesus as our Savior, we join a new family ... "God´s family". This is one of the biggest gifts we receive. Now we have a Heavenly Father and many brothers and sisters in Jesus Christ. If you are the only Christian in your earthly family, you shouldn't feel alone because you have a big spiritual family.

The Apostle Paul says in Ephesians 2:19, "Consequently, you are no longer foreigners and aliens, but fellow citizen with God´s people and members of God´s household." The family we belong to is the church.

# What does the word "Church" mean?

There is a lot of confusion related to what the word "church" means. Some people say, "let's go to church" referring to the place or building where Christian people gather together. When the Bible uses the word "church," it means people who have received new life in Christ. In other words, they are God´s sons and daughters.

Therefore, the church is not the place or building where the believers gather together to worship God, but the group of persons who have believed and accepted Jesus as their Lord and Savior.

The word "church" just means "assembly," and the New Testament writers use the term to refer to the followers of the Lord Jesus. When we talk about "church," we may refer to a congregation of believers from a certain community (called a "local church" as well); or to a group of believers who gather together in a house or another place; or to the "universal church", which is the total of believers around the world, including those who have died, whose names are written in the eternal book of life (Philippians 4:3). The church is local as well as universal.

Different than any other community or organization, the church is a "living" organism. The Bible says that it is the body of Christ, and all who have accepted the call to be followers of Jesus are part of that body.

The Church of the Nazarene is part of this great universal church, and has as its important objectives, "holy Christian fellowship, the conversion of sinners, the entire sanctification of believers, their up building in holiness, and the simplicity and spiritual power manifest in the primitive New Testament Church, together with the preaching of the gospel to every creature." (Nazarene Church Manual)

## How was the church born?

God created man and woman to live in a perfect relationship with Him. However, humans decided to turn their backs on God, go their own way, and become enemies of their Creator.

This intention of becoming their own gods, and refusing God's sovereignty over their lives, took them into a life of slavery under the domain of sin and all its consequences, including death and eternal suffering far from God's presence. The Bible tells us that God took the initiative, and in his great love looked for all the possible ways of liberating people from sin's slavery.

God formed a nation to announce to the world his love, mercy and salvation. That was the reason why God looked for and called Abraham (Genesis 12:1-9), to raise up through him a great nation that would announce to all the people of the earth not only the horrible consequences of sin, but also the good news of salvation from sin. In time, Abraham's descendants ended up becoming the great nation of Israel, but regrettably, it moved away from the purpose for which God formed them. To help them, God sent his servants, the prophets, who announced that God would form a new nation that would serve him. That nation is the church that our Lord Jesus founded. (1 Peter 2:9-10)

The church came from God´s heart. He sent his son Jesus Christ to give his life as a sacrifice, and in this way became the Lord and master of the church. It's nice to know that God´s love for each one of us is the reason why He gave his own son to die on the cross. And just as the Father gave himself to Jesus Christ, in the same way Jesus Christ gave himself for the church "to make her holy, cleansing her with the washing of water by the word" (Ephesians 5:25-26). Having been purchased by the blood of Jesus, and receiving Him as Savior, you and I belong to him. God is Lord and Master of us, His church (1 Corinthians 6:20).

The historical moment that is marked as the launch of the Christian Church to the world is the Day of Pentecost (Acts 2). The church began its ministry baptized with the power of the Holy Spirit. Christ had promised the Holy Spirit to his disciples (John 16:5-16). The Spirit of God gives power to the church for living in obedience to God´s Word and for carrying out the purpose for why it was put into this world.

# The Unity of the Church

Paul affirms in 1 Corinthians 12:27 that the church is Christ's Body, "Now you are the body of Christ, and individual members of it." He also affirms this in Colossians 1:18, "He is also the head of the body, the church." Christ is the head, not only in the sense of being the one who gives origin or life to the church, but also because he is the one who governs and guides it. Therefore, if we are united to Christ, we are also united to each other, and we have a responsibility to and for each other."

This comparison between the church and the human body helps us understand clearly the great diversity that exists among the people who make up the church. The hands have their own function. A foot works in coordination with the other foot. The eyes, ears, mouth, and each part of the body has an important function, and depends on one of the others for its survival. All the parts of the body exist together equally, not one being better than the other. In the same way, the members of God's body must respect and accept each other, helping each other grow.

On the other hand, when we say the church is only one body, we realize that the church should not be considered only as a numeric group of believers or small groups of isolated believers. The church is to be a united community that gathers for worship. The church shares common bonds of spiritual life, suffering, commitment, faith and service. The local church consists of each local group of believers.

Christ is the one who gives growth to the church as the members cooperate. "From him the whole body, joined and held together by every supporting ligament, grows and builds itself up in love, as each part does its work." (Ephesians 4:16)

Jesus Christ wants the church to be united (John 17:21). This doesn't require a combining of all the churches or local groups, but it suggests the existence of a common purpose. We can only have true unity if we come closer to Christ, preach his Gospel, and live as he would live in our place.

# The Purpose for the Existence of the Church in the World:

If the church is a divine creation founded by Christ and composed of all those who have received new life in Christ, why was it created? The Bible teaches us that God has also given to his people special abilities called gifts. He has given these gifts for his people to carry out a special service or purpose for which God has called him or her. God's purposes for his church are explained in the Great Commandment and The Great Commission (Mathew 22:37-40, 28:18-20). These purposes can be grouped in 5 areas: Worship, Fellowship, Evangelism, Discipleship, and Training for service. Let's see what each one of these purposes consists of.

**Worship**. God is looking for people who will worship him (John 4:23) and love him over everything else (Mathew 4:10). Everything we do, individually or as church, should be an act of worship where God can show his glory to the world (1 Corinthians 10:31). God has called us to be a "sacrifice of praise" (Hebrews 13:15). The Bible instructs us to talk with other believers with "psalms, hymns, and spiritual songs" (Ephesians 5:19). When we meet as the church, we pray and listen to God´s Word. These are forms of worship. We also worship when we participate together in Communion and Baptism of new believers.

**Fellowship.** The word "fellowship" means companionship. Jesus calls his disciples "friends" (John 15:14). In fact, this friendship with Jesus is what made the church into a community of love and care - a community that was willing to share with each other. Love for one another should be the distinctive mark of the church (John 13:35).

**Evangelism**. God has saved us to "proclaim the praises of the One who called you out of darkness into His marvelous light" (1 Peter 2:9). Gospel means the announcement of the good news of salvation that God has provided in Christ. People who don't yet belong to God´s people have many needs of all types, and we shouldn't ignore them. But the biggest need that people have is to hear the Gospel and accept the good news of salvation. People need more than ever to have a face to face encounter with God´s love. They need to have God in their lives. As the church of Christ, our principal service to the world is preaching the good news of salvation. No other organization does this work. This is the exclusive mission of the church. All believers must be involved in the work of the gospel. Some people will evangelize by inviting their friends to church, home Bible studies, prayer cells, or family groups. Others evangelize by testifying to what God has done in their lives or by preaching the Good News. Others contribute with finances as gifts of God´s love. Others present the good news by giving clothes or food to those in need, or by taking care of sick people. Some people share through music or other ministries in the church. We must do this together as the body of Christ. By participating and being together, God will help many people to be saved and His church will grow (1 Corinthians 3:5-9, Ephesians 4:16).

**Discipleship.** Teaching new believers is the center of the Great Commission that the Lord Jesus entrusted to all his followers, "teaching them to obey everything I have commanded you" (Mathew 28:20). Every member of the church is responsible for sharing what he has learned with others (1 Corinthians 14:31, 1 Thessalonians 5:11, Hebrews 10:25). One effective way of teaching is through small group Bible studies. These provide an excellent atmosphere for this mutual ministry (service).

The apostle Paul refers to this teaching when he affirms that we should "build up the church" (1 Corinthians 14:12). We do this when we gather together, when we encourage, when we comfort each other (v.3), etc. Every meeting of the church must be for building up the body (v.26). In the church, we are all to be disciples. A disciple is a person who learns and applies God´s Word to his daily life. The early church was recognized in the community where they lived because "they devoted themselves to the apostles teaching, to the fellowship, to the breaking of bread, and to prayer" (Acts 2:42).

**Training for service.** The second greatest commandment is about loving one's neighbor (Mathew 22:39). Paul writes: "Therefore, as we have opportunity, we must work for the good of all, especially for those who belong to the household of faith" (Galatians 6:10). Our obligation is to help the rest of the people in their needs. Help the people who are closest to us, like our family in the flesh and brothers and sisters of God´s family, as well as help the person who lives in the furthest place. Therefore, all Christians should be trained so that we can put to good use the abilities and talents that God has given to us. It's the responsibility of the church to train every believer so that they can be actively involved in the ministry to which God has called them and enabled them with gifts of the Spirit. Every Christian has a vocation in Christ and a call to service. (Mathew 28:18-20)

## Why do We Need to Belong to a Local Church?

There are many people who are Christians but who don't want to be part of a church. These people cheat themselves because the New Testament clearly states that Christians are to gather together. (Hebrews 10:25)

The apostle Paul repeatedly encourages Christians to have fellowship with each other, to encourage one another, and have friendship with each other. This is almost impossible if the believers do not gather together (Romans 12:10, 15:7, 1 Corinthians 12:25, Galatians 5:13, Ephesians 4:32, Philippians 2:3, Colossians 3:13, 1 Thessalonians 5:13). In the church, we find a place where we learn how to serve.

Another reason why we need to belong to a local church is because it gives us a sense of belonging to a group that supports us and helps us to stay in biblical truth and not dragged away by strange ideas. In the church, we learn truths that otherwise we couldn't learn for ourselves. We also receive practical valuable advice for confronting difficult situations in our lives.

Being a part of the church permits us to receive the care of our pastors and brothers and sisters in the faith. They watch out for our progress and perseverance in Christian life and discipleship. We must remember that we have started a new spiritual life, and we need to grow day by day. When we are new believers, we require care and attention according to our needs. It is for that reason that each of the meetings and ministries of the church are instruments that God uses to help us in our life.

However, the most important reason for which each believer should participate in a local church is because the church needs the believer. The new believer is affirmed in her Christian life as she is involved more and more in the ministries of the church. When believers are not involved in the work of the church, the healthy growth of the church suffers gravely in all areas (1Corinthians 12:4-7).

Finally, as members of a church, we also have the privilege of contributing to the ministry of the church in our local community and throughout the world through our offerings and tithes (Malachi 3:10). These gifts of love to the church are part of our worship to God as we share with others from the blessings He has given to us. The church is a family where we help each other. And in that mutual help we have the privilege of serving God with all that we are and all that He has given us.

## Why do Christians Gather Together on Sundays?

From the time of the creation of the world, according to the command of God, believers have dedicated one day of the week to rest, worship and the learning of God´s Word. This day was called the Sabbath, or day of rest. God commanded this because He rested from his work of creation on the seventh day (Genesis 2:2-3).

In the fourth of the Ten Commandments, God commands, "Remember the Sabbath and keep it holy." The rest that was established by God has a sacred value. God invites people not only to rest physically, but also to rest "in the Lord." We rest in the Lord by praising him, by giving him thanks, and having an intimacy of love with Him.

The Christians of the New Testament celebrated the resurrection of the Lord Jesus Christ on Sunday (John 20:26; Acts 20:7; 1 Corinthians 16:2, Revelation 1:10). This celebration took the place of the Sabbath rest that had been on Saturday. Now Sunday is called "the day of the Lord."

It was Sunday as well that began to mark the rhythm of the life of the Christians. The first Christians specifically dedicated the first day of the week to worshiping the Lord, having communion with each other, and participating together in worshiping God as his people.

That´s why Sunday is the day that Jesus Christ's followers are called to remember the salvation that they have received thanks to Jesus' sacrifice. That´s the reason for celebration for the Christian. And it´s not only a memory of an event that happened a long time ago, but also the trust that the resurrected Jesus Christ is with his disciples now ("for where two or three are gathered together in My name, I am there among them" - Mathew 18:20), and he will come to be with them forever (Mathew 28:20).

## How Can I Join the Church?

Christ's church is composed of all the people who have received new life in Jesus Christ. Therefore, to be able to be part of the church, we need to be born again by admitting and regretting our sins, accepting Christ as our personal Savior, and recognizing him as our Lord.

To be a member of a Church of the Nazarene, we should declare openly the experience of our salvation, believe firmly in the biblical truths that the church teaches, and commit to participate actively in the ministries of the church with its leaders and pastors.

## Conclusion

Think about a boy who has lived without the affection of his parents since he was a child, maybe looking every day where to spend the night, many times without something to eat. And suddenly, a man appears in his life telling him, "Come with me. I want to provide you with a home, a place where you will have the father´s love and the affection of many people who, like you, have suffered a long time, but today enjoy his protection, a place to sleep, food, and affection... of a family."

Possibly if you were that boy, you wouldn't believe it. It would not be easy to understand why someone would make this gracious offer to you. However, it´s true. That´s God's plan for you. "God loved us so much that He decided to send Jesus Christ to adopt us as his children, because he had planned this from the beginning" (Ephesians 1:4-6).

Being a member of the family of God is a great privilege that we don't deserve. When receiving him, we must make a commitment to attract everyone we can to our new family, the church. We make this in partnership with the body of Christ through the power of the Holy Spirit.

# Notes:

# DISCOVERING JESUS EVERY DAY
## 31 devotionals for new Christians in the Gospel of Luke

**Christian Sarmiento**
**Mónica E. Mastronardi de Fernández**

## Luke 1:1-25    Day 1

*"Both of them were righteous in the sight of God, observing all the Lord's commands and decrees righteously."*
Luke 1:6

This passage shows us the example of Zachariah and Elisabeth:

1. They were righteous before God. God has made you righteous. When He makes us righteous, He cleanses us of sin, we become "right" before Him. Now you are a different person because God has cleansed your sins through Christ's blood. Some people you know who are not Christians don't understand this, and might expect you to return to the sins of the past. But in Christ we are righteous, even when others don't understand us.

2. They obeyed all the commandments and ordinances. They were obedient to God. By reading and understanding God's Word, we can live in obedience and be examples to other people.

**Examine yourself:** Do I want with all my heart to grow up in the new life that Christ has given me? Am I setting aside time every day for reading the Bible and praying?

**Pray:** Father, help me to persevere in reading your Word. With the help of the Holy Spirit and the leaders of my church, I will apply your Word in all the areas of my life.

# Luke 1:26-56

*"I am the Lord's servant," Mary answered.*
*"May your word to me be fulfilled." Luke 1:38*

1. God had a plan for Mary's life. She was chosen by God for a special purpose. He carried out his purpose in Mary because she was submissive and obedient to God's will. She unconditionally put her life in the hands of the Lord. She didn't ask for money, fame, power or any other personal benefit in exchange for her obedience to the Lord.

2. God has a purpose for your life, just like God had a plan for Mary's life, He has a purpose for each person. When you unconditionally place your life in God's hands, He will make his purpose known to you. In the plans that God has for you, He will bless you, and at the same time, He will bless others through you.

**Examine yourself:** Am I willing to follow the plan that God has prepared for my life?

**Pray:** Lord, make me a disciple willing to serve you in all that you request from me. Thank you for creating a plan for my life so that I can be a blessing to others.

# Luke 1:57-80

*"Immediately his mouth was opened and his tongue set free, and he began to speak, praising God." Luke 1:64*

1. Zachariah had many reasons to praise God. One was that God had given a son to him and his sterile wife in their old age. God had revealed to Zachariah the special plan that He had for his son John - that John the Baptist would prepare the hearts of the people for the arrival of Jesus the Savior. God punished Zachariah for not believing His miracle by making him speechless for nine months. Now, God healed him and he could tell of God's marvels to many others.

2. You also have reasons to praise God. God has given you a new life in Christ Jesus. That's the Good News that you can share with others. The blessings that we receive from God are to be shared with everyone. The gospel is the good news that there is eternal life in Christ Jesus. Everyone you know needs to hear the gospel from you.

**Examine yourself:** What reasons do I have today to praise God?

**Pray:** Lord I praise you for the good things that you have done in my life! Help me to share this good news with my friends and family.

# Luke 2:1-52 `Day 4`

*"But the angel said to them, 'Do not be afraid. I bring you good news that will cause great joy for all the people. Today in the town of David a Savior has been born to you; he is the Messiah, the Lord.'" Luke 2:10-11*

1.  We have a Savior! Jesus came to save us from ourselves, forgiving us of our sin. He came to save our family and our friends. He is the Savior of the world!

2.  Jesus is Christ and Lord. The word "Christ" points to the liberator sent by God. We have a liberator. This is great news that brings joy to the heart. In Christ there is hope. When Christ comes again, there won't be any pain or sadness. We'll be eternally with Him. That's our hope!

3.  The word "Lord" means owner, the one who has control. The best thing that someone can do is give Jesus the control of his life. Then He will guide us step by step in all our decisions. This will bring glory to God, and others will want to have the life and salvation that we enjoy.

**Examine yourself:** Am I allowing Christ to be Lord of all areas of my life?

**Pray:** Thank you Father for sending your son Jesus to this world to be my Savior and my Lord. Today I give you total control of my life.

# Luke 3:1-38 `Day 5`

*"and the Holy Spirit descended on him in bodily form like a dove. And a voice came from heaven: 'You are my Son, whom I love; with you I am well pleased.' " Luke 3:22*

Baptism is a public testimony of what God has done in your life. Christians are baptized because this was commanded by our Lord Jesus. When we are baptized, we affirm that we want to live as Christ's disciples.

1. You are a beloved child of God. Now you can come to God in prayer with the same trust that a son comes to his loving father. The only ones who have the right to call upon God the Father are those who have accepted Christ as his or her personal Savior.

2. The Father delights in having you as His child. When a person regrets his or her sins and lives in Christ Jesus, God is happy and feels satisfied with his new child.

**Examine yourself:** Am I experiencing in my life the joy of being a child of God? Do I want to be baptized, as Jesus was, to demonstrate my desire to be his disciple?

**Pray:** Lord, my desire is to follow you by being baptized.

# Luke 4:1-14 `Day 6`

*"Jesus, full of the Holy Spirit, . . . was tempted . . . Jesus returned to Galilee in the power of the Spirit." Luke 4:1,2,14*

To be tempted is normal. Every human being, including our Lord Jesus, is tempted. His strategy for conquering temptation was to reject it immediately. So what is the key for us to conquer temptation?

We are not victorious by our discipline or by our strength of character. Sooner or later, temptation defeats our human limitations. Neither is it education. Nothing that we do in our own strength will guarantee us victory over temptation. God's Word teaches us that we should flee from temptation. The Christian should stay away from thoughts, places, entertainment and situations that present temptation. But he can't do it without God's help.

The only thing that can guarantee us victory is to be filled with the presence of the Holy Spirit. Now He personally lives in you. You need to depend on Him to conquer temptations and have a victorious life.

**Examine yourself:** What are the temptations that harass me?

**Pray:** Lord, please fill me with your Holy Spirit  and help me conquer the temptations that harass me. Give me the willpower to flee from what you don't like.

# Luke 4:14-44 `Day 7`

*"They were amazed at his teaching, because his words had authority." Luke 4:32*

Why did the people say that Jesus spoke with authority? Not because He screamed or imposed his point of view. Not because He forced them to obey his words.

The authority of Jesus resided in the fact that He spoke with the truth of the Scriptures. Jesus presented the Scriptures of the Old Testament to teach them about who He was.

Jesus was the fulfillment of the promises of the Old Testament. Jesus is living proof that we can fully trust in the promises of God. God doesn't lie; neither has He taken back any of His promises. Christ is the living Word of God. He is the safest rock to which we can anchor our life.

**Examine yourself:** In what or whom have I placed my trust? In my profession? In my possessions? In my strength? In my family? Or in Christ?

**Pray:** Lord, thank you for being a God who always tells me the truth. Help me to value your Word as the unique and true guide for my life. Help me to live in the truth.

# Luke 5:1:39 `Day 8`

*"Then Jesus said to Simon, 'Don't be afraid; from now on you will fish for people.' " Luke 5:10*

What occupation do you have? Carpenter? Doctor? Bank Teller? Secretary? Professor/Teacher? Do you work in a factory or an office? Now that you are a Christian, you have a new occupation: fisher of people. Jesus told Peter, "Now you will be a fisher of people." The word "fisherman" indicates that one should catch something that is alive. Jesus wants you to have a second profession. He doesn't want you to give up your job. He wants you to continue in that job where you are to fish for people.

Christ's disciples have the privilege of sharing the new life in Christ with other people. That's the meaning of testimony: To tell others, with my own words and my example, about the hope of salvation in Christ. Jesus wants your life to shine so strong that those around you will notice the difference that Christ makes in you. Just like bait helps the fishermen attract fish, God will use your life to attract many others for eternal salvation in Christ.

**Examine yourself:** Is my life today a living example so that others may know Christ as their personal Savior?

**Pray:** Lord, thanks for this opportunity that you give me to be your collaborator for the salvation of others.

# Luke 6:1-11 `Day 9`

*"Then Jesus said to them, 'The Son of Man is Lord of the Sabbath.' " Luke 6:5*

Since the creation of the world, God has told us to keep one day to rest. This day will be devoted to the exclusive service of God. Israel kept Saturday. In Jesus' days, the Jews took this commandment to the extreme, even prohibiting people from doing good for others on the day of rest. But, Jesus and his disciples taught, healed and assisted the needy on that day. For this reason they were criticized. Jesus is the one who should tell us how to use this day. As Christians, we should help others every day, even on Sundays, which is our day of rest. Jesus hopes we give an important part of our time to serve him completely.

Christians gather together on Sundays to worship God and learn from His Word. The Christian participates in the ministries of the church on Sundays. But, the church also has ministries on other days of the week as well. These offers service opportunities to help the community and other believers.

**Examine yourself:** Am I setting aside an important part of my time to serve God by serving others?

**Pray:** Lord, thanks for teaching us to set aside a day for you. Help me to be organized so that I can dedicate a good amount of time to serve you every week.

## Luke 6:12-49 `Day 10`

*"As for everyone who comes to me and hears my words and puts them into practice, I will show you what they are like. They are like . . ." Luke 6:47-48*

Whom do you want to be like? Our life model is Christ - we live to imitate Him. We were made in His likeness (Genesis 1:27). Jesus lives in you and you should allow him to be shown in your life. How? The key is obedience. Obedience is hearing His Word, and immediately doing what He says. The obedient person is compared to a man who built his house on a sure foundation. This firm house represents the Christian's life whose foundation is Christ.

We all have problems in our lives. There isn't anybody who can escape from them. But when problems arrive in the believer's life, our life will be on the rock that is Christ (1 Corinthians 10:4). If you live your life in Christ, people who are around you each day will see the truth of your testimony. They will see that your life is built on the Rock, Jesus. It doesn't matter how severe the storm is, He will always sustain you.

**Examine yourself:** How do you react to problems?

**Pray:** Lord, help me to be obedient to your Word, even when the problems come.

## Luke 7:1-50 `Day 11`

*"When Jesus heard this, he was amazed at him, . . .'I tell you, I have not found such great faith.'" Luke 7:9*

Our relationship with Jesus is by means of faith. Faith is trusting in what is expected, still believing even when it cannot be verified by the senses (Hebrews 11:1). We cannot see Jesus like people that lived in the first century. But He is alive and He is real. He listens to our prayers and provides for our needs. It doesn't matter what our needs are, He helps us and He gives an answer, "yes", "no", or "later." We should trust that he knows what we need.

Our faith to ask for a special favor from God should be in Him and not in some other human being. The Christian life is a life of faith. Deposit all your faith in Jesus and you will see results. God promises in his Word, "...trust in Him and He will do this" (Psalm 37:5).

**Examine yourself:** Am I putting my faith in Jesus or in somebody else? To whom do I give the credit when God answers my prayer?

**Pray:** Lord, thanks for giving us the gift of faith. Help me to trust you completely and to pray for those who need you. My prayer is that you can show your love to them.

# Luke 8:1-21

*"and also some women . . . and many others. These women were helping to support them out of their own means." Luke 8:2,3*

"The earth is the LORD's, and everything in it, the world, and all who live in it; for he founded it on the seas and established it on the waters." (Psalm 24:1, 2). All things that exist belong to God and we have the privilege of collaborating with Him in the care of His creation. Equally we have been put by God in his world and we enjoy all that comes from Him. As God's children, we should take care of the things that he has given us. What we have should be used to meet our needs and to help others that are in need.

The Christian's motivation to give is not from duty, interest or the fear of punishment. We give out of love and gratitude to God who generously has given to us everything, "Jesus Christ, ... he became poor, so that you through his poverty might become rich" (2 Corinthians 8:9). This is the attitude that God expects from us in terms of our time, abilities and possessions.

**Examine yourself:** What does the example of these women teach me in terms of the attitude with which I should serve the Lord? Is there some way that I can serve the Lord today?

**Pray:** Lord, show me how to serve you with my life and with all that you have given me. Give me a generous heart.

# Luke 8:22-56

*"Jesus said, 'Don't be afraid; just believe, and she will be healed.'" Lk 8:50*

Here we find four crises in the lives of these people. The disciples, trapped on the lake in a storm, thought they weren't going to survive. A young person, tormented by a demon, who lived rejected by people, loveless and without hope. A woman suffering a shameful and incurable sickness that had left her poor. And parents from whom death had taken their daughter.

We all go through situations that make us feel desperate. But when we face the suffering, Jesus is with us. God is our best ally to face problems. He wants to guide us to find the best solution. Sometimes we trust in ourselves or in others and not in Christ. You are the only person who can move towards God and away from yourself. Don't move away from God when you're suffering. Without God, the pain becomes unbearable and it seems that problems don't have solutions.

**Examine yourself**: Is there some situation that causes me anguish that I should put in God's hands today?

**Pray:** Lord, I put this situation in your hands ... please give me wisdom and comfort.

# Luke 9:1-24

*"For whoever wants to save their life will lose it, but whoever loses their life for me will save it." Luke 9:24*

Who wants to lose his or her life? No one. Our life is our most valuable treasure. Then, which life is Jesus speaking of? What is the life that we should lose?

The life that we should lose is the independence from God, i.e., my projects, my dreams, my desires, etc. The one who keeps this life will literally lose everything. When committing everything to Jesus, I ask him to show me His projects, His dreams, and His desires for my life. If I follow his will for my life, this will give me all that I need. I will make a difference in this world, and save my life. You should remember, Jesus came and gave his life for you. Now it's your chance to give him all. When you do that, Jesus will give his love to others through us. When we totally surrender to God, He responds by filling us with his Spirit, so that he dwells in us and fills each of us. God's Spirit teaches us to live an obedient life to God, following Jesus' example. (Luke 11.13)

**Examine yourself:** Do I want to respond to Jesus with total surrender, or is there some part of my life that still remains mine?

**Pray:** Father, I want my life to be completely yours, filled with your Spirit through my entire being. My life is completely yours, my Lord. Use me as you please.

# Luke 10:42

*"He told them, 'The harvest is plentiful, but the workers are few. Ask the Lord of the harvest, therefore, to send out workers into his harvest field.' " Luke 10:2*

God needs workers for his harvest. The word "harvest" refers to a field or crop that is ready to be reaped or gathered. If there are no workers to reap or pick the crop at the time that it is ripe, the crop is lost. In this passage, the crop is humanity that is ready to listen and grow in the new life that is in Christ Jesus.

There are many types of workers who serve in the church: Bible teachers, preachers, musicians, evangelists, among others. There are so many people who need to hear about Jesus! It is for that reason that a few workers are not enough. God needs for you to share his concern for the shortage of workers. Start praying to the Lord of the harvest to send workers, and get ready to respond to the Lord when He asks you to serve Him. Whatever your profession is, God can use you for the harvest. For this, He has given you abilities, a profession, and life experience so that you can share Jesus with those who are ready to listen.

**Examine yourself:** How can God use me to bring more workers to his harvest?

**Pray:** Lord, I want to be part of your harvest, to talk to people who have not heard yet, so that they can know that there is new life in Jesus.

# Luke 11:1-54 `Day 16`

*"Forgive us our sins, for we also forgive
everyone who sins against us . . ." Luke 11:4*

Jesus constantly prayed. Praying was as natural for Jesus as breathing. When Jesus taught his disciples how to pray (Luke 11:2-4), he did it using simple words. God doesn't expect prepared speeches from us. He hopes that we will come to him in confidence. The Lord's Prayer teaches us to pray as members of the church. The church is made up of God's children who accept Jesus as their Lord. The task of the church is to expand God's kingdom in our communities. God's kingdom is present where we are because God reigns in our hearts. In this kingdom, God's will is fully obeyed.

God's will is that we are one. God wants us to forgive one another and in this way, to be united in Him. It's for that reason that, every day, we should forgive those who offend us by their words or actions.

**Examine yourself:** Is there something in my heart that I need to forgive? Has someone hurt me with his or her words, attitude or behavior? Do I believe that God can give me enough love to forgive this person?

**Pray:** Lord, I want to forgive in the same way that you forgive me.

# Luke 12:1-57 `Day 17`

*"Where your treasure is, there your heart will be also." Luke 12:34*

In Jesus' day, as well as today, the heart represents the center of our intellect and our moral conscience and decisions.

What is a treasure? It is something that we value a lot and don't want to lose. It is something that we love and it may represent our hope for the future. Generally, we are ready to defend our treasure at any cost. If caring for our treasures requires all of our attention and energy, we are giving them more importance than they should have.

God wants to be the top priority in our life, so that nothing distracts us from our service and relationship to Him. When we don't give God first place in our heart, other things end up absorbing all our time, energy, thoughts and love away from Him. If we don't give first place to God, Satan will fill our lives with other things.

**Examine yourself:** Write a list of your treasures.

**Pray:** Lord, I want to give you first place in my life, and make the rest of my list secondary to your reign.

# Luke 13:1-35 `Day 18`

*"But when Jesus saw her, He called her forward and said to her, 'Woman, you are set free from your infirmity.' " Luke 13:12*

Jesus' Words have the ability to heal internally and externally. Whatever your need is, Jesus has the power to heal you. On occasion, the healing happens in an instant. Other times, the healing comes later in the process of restoration. On other occasions, healing doesn't arrive until after physical death, like the case of the Apostle Paul. (2 Corinthians 12:7)

The salvation that God offers is complete! He wants to restore us from all the marks that sin has left on our life. This salvation work begins at the moment in which we receive new life in Christ Jesus, and it continues throughout our lifetime. In this process, God restores us to his image and likeness.

**Examine yourself:** Is there some physical or emotional disease of which I need to be healed? Is there some other person that needs health for their body and life?

**Pray:** Lord, I ask you to heal me of the sickness from which I suffer. I know this is possible thanks to Christ's sacrifice on the cross for me. Now I intercede, also, for _____, so that he or she will experience your healing, and that they can also know you as their personal Savior.

# Luke 14:1-34 `Day 19`

*"In the same way, those of you who do not give up everything you have cannot be my disciples." Luke 14:33*

The key to this verse is the word "be". A disciple is someone who lives exactly like his master. Then, we may wonder, how did Jesus live?

In the book of Philippians, the Apostle Paul responds to this question by saying that Jesus "made himself nothing, by taking the very nature of a servant ... he humbled himself by becoming obedient to death ..." (Philippians 2:7, 8) Thanks to the perfect obedience of Jesus, we can be his disciples and have eternal life. To be a disciple, it is necessary to follow Jesus. How? By being like him and doing what He did.

• By giving our life totally to God ("he made himself nothing")
• By giving our life in service to others ("he humbled himself by becoming obedient to death...")

The key to being a disciple is to give up our rights to ourselves and to persevere in following Christ.

**Examine yourself:** Do I resemble Jesus more and more in my way of living? What have I given up to follow Jesus?

**Pray:** Heavenly Father, please make me into a disciple who lives as my Lord and Teacher, Jesus. Please change in me everything that hinders me from being like Him.

# Luke 15:1-32

*"In the same way, I tell you, there is rejoicing in the presence of the angels of God over one sinner who repents." Luke 15:10*

Jesus liked to use parables to teach spiritual truths. A parable is a story. It can be a true story or it may be a story that is based on real life situations. In Luke 15, we find 3 parables about lost objects: a sheep, a coin and a son.

All people lose something at some time. Something that is lost is something that isn't in the right place. The Bible teaches us that Jesus "came to seek and to save the lost..." (Luke 19:10). That is why Christ came. If someone doesn't know Christ, he is lost. Jesus wants us to follow the example of the shepherd who searched for his lost sheep (v. 4-7), and the woman who searched for her lost coin (v. 8-10), and the father who kept watch for his lost son. We are to search for those who are far from Christ. God is the loving Father who is waiting for his lost children to come to Him. (v. 12-32)

**Examine yourself:** Write the names of 5 lost people you know.

1. _____
2. _____
3. _____
4. _____
5. _____

**Pray:** My God, please give me opportunity to give my testimony about what you've done in my life to these people.

# Luke 16:1-18

*"Anyone who divorces his wife and marries another woman commits adultery, and the man who marries a divorced woman commits adultery." Luke 16:18*

God doesn't want his children to be guided by the norms and customs that are accepted by most people when those norms go against His will. In Jesus' days, men were entitled to the legal right of getting divorced from their wife for any reason. Today, divorce is accepted and practiced in many countries as a simple way to end the sacred union of marriage. Some people marry thinking that if the relationship doesn't go well, there is an easy solution. The breakup of the marriage bond is one of the most destructive experiences for spouses and their children.

Some people become disciples of Christ after they have already divorced and started a new relationship. God doesn't continue to blame us for the bad decisions that we make while we were far from Him. God forgives us when we accept Christ as our Savior but wants us to be accountable for our decisions and commitments from now on.

**Examine yourself:** Am I a person of my word? Am I doing what I promise? Do I keep my commitments?

**Pray:** Lord, please help me to be a reliable person, so that others can see Christ in me.

# Luke 16:19-30

*"In Hades, where he was in torment, he looked up and saw Abraham far away, with Lazarus by his side." Luke 16:23*

"Hades" is the name Jews give to the place where people who have done bad things in God's eyes go after they die. We know Hades as Hell, and it is a place of eternal punishment. Some people have the hope that when they die, they will have an opportunity to go to an intermediate place, called purgatory. But this popular belief doesn't have a biblical base.

The Bible only gives two options: heaven or hell. Heaven is for those that have followed Christ faithfully. Hell is for Satan, demons and those that reject Christ. They are very different places. In heaven, there is eternal peace and joy in God's presence. In hell there is torment and sadness forever. Jesus helps us by asking, "Where do you want to spend eternity?" The answer to this question will tell us how we are going to live from now on.

**Examine yourself:** Am I getting ready to live for eternity with God, or away from God?

**Pray:** Thank you Lord for inviting me to live eternally with you. Please help me to always live near you until the day that I'll be in your presence forever.

# Luke 17:1-37

*"Even if they sin against you seven times in a day and seven times come back to you saying 'I repent,' you must forgive them." Luke 17:4*

If we want to grow in Christ and be his disciples, we must do what Jesus asks of us. One of the most difficult practices is forgiveness. It's like a double sided coin. Jesus says, "But if you do not forgive, neither will your Father who is in heaven forgive your sins" (Mark 11:26).

It not only refers to forgiving those who don't have a close relationship with us, the command is also for those situations in which it is very difficult to forgive. When our friends and loved ones harm us, our feelings are hurt and it's hard to forgive. There is no limit to forgiveness. The key is to forgive, to forgive, and to forgive. Jesus uses the number seven to insinuate that it should be a total forgiveness. When we don't forgive, our lives become filled with bitterness.

**Examine yourself:** Am I keeping in my heart something against another person who has offended me by word or action?

**Pray:** Lord, please help me to forgive _____, and clean my life of all bitterness and spite. Help me to always forgive those who hurt me.

## Luke 18:1-43

*"For all those who exalt themselves will be humbled, and those who humble themselves will be exalted." Luke 18:14*

The humility that is applauded in this passage is not poverty. A person can be poor and at the same time proud. This humility is "modesty." It is the attitude of one who does things because they love people and not for applause or recognition. It is the one who helps others grow, even when no one notices what he or she does.

The proud/arrogant do not approach God with the correct attitude. He says, "I don't need anyone, I'm self-sufficient." The proud treat God as if they don't need Him. Instead, the humble person says, "My God, how can I serve you?"

The humble person sees himself as a slave of God and of his fellowman. This was Jesus' attitude when he offered us the biggest service that somebody could give us, when he died on the cross in our place.

**Examine yourself:** Is my attitude of prayer, of humility, as God expects of me?

**Pray:** Lord, please give me a humble heart, free of pride and conceit. Help me to serve You so that You are glorified, instead of looking for honors for myself.

## Luke 19:1-48

*"Zacchaeus, come down immediately. I must stay at your house today." Luke 19:5*

Zacchaeus was a very busy man in his business. He had earned a lot of money and few friends. One day, Zacchaeus looked to move away from the routine and tried to see the man of whom everybody was speaking. But he didn't know that Jesus would change his life. Jesus didn't only want to have a moment with him, but he wanted also to enter his home and have a friendship with him. In the same way, Jesus wants to be a friend of each one of us, and He wants us to introduce our friends to Him.

Zacchaeus' life became very different from the day he accepted Jesus as his friend. The friends that we appreciate most are those who know how to give us good advice. Zacchaeus understood that he had acted badly in his business, so he distributed to the poor the money that he had unjustly taken from them. Jesus wants to guide us to fix the mistakes of our past.

**Examine yourself:** Am I allowing Jesus to be my Friend? Am I putting into practice what Jesus tells me that I should do or not do?

**Pray:** Lord Jesus, I want you to be my friend and live in my life. Please help me to seek your guidance before I make decisions.

# Luke 20:1-47

*"He said to them, 'Then give back to Caesar what is Caesar's, and to God what is God's.' " Luke 20:25*

The religious leaders tried to set traps for Jesus so that they would have a motive to kill him. They asked him questions with bad intentions. In this passage, they asked him if it was good to disobey the Roman emperor by refusing to pay taxes. If Jesus answered that it was not necessary to pay them, they would report him to the Romans. If Jesus answered that they should pay taxes, he would be unpopular with the people, because the Romans were the invaders who had taken away their national independence. So, what belongs to Caesar and what belongs to God? They knew the answer, but they were not willing to put it into practice.

Paul says in Romans 12:1, "offer your bodies as a living sacrifice..." God wants us to serve Him with all our being, AND to fulfill our duties as citizens.

**Examine yourself:** Have I had to face traps from some people who don't accept my new life in Christ at this time?

**Pray:** Lord, please help me to be wise in knowing how to respond to people who make fun of me and You.

# Luke 21:1-38

*"Stand firm, and you will win life." Luke 21:19*

Here Jesus spoke of two future events. This is known as prophecy. First (v. 7-24), he warns them of the destruction of the city of Jerusalem that would happen 50 years after his death, in the year 70 AD. Then, Jesus spoke of events that would precede his second coming (v. 25-38). Jesus recommended that they be patient when those things happened.

Mark 13:13 says, "the one who stands firm to the end will be saved." To persevere is to stay firm in spite of the circumstances that want to stop us. Patience helps us to persevere in our faithfulness to the Lord. Problems are inevitable but a tribulation is more than a problem. A tribulation is a time of affliction so big that it is almost impossible to stand. In those moments, some people blame God and move away from him. But it is exactly in those moments when we need to be near God the most.

**Examine yourself:** Am I facing any problems that can move me away from Jesus?

**Pray:** Lord, please help me to keep my eyes on you and not on the problems. I always want to be near you.

# Luke 22:1-30

*"This cup is the new covenant in My blood,
which is poured out for you." Luke 22:20*

A "covenant" is a commitment between two parties. Now days, we use the word "contract" instead of "covenant" to buy property, to do work, etc. But Jesus speaks of a new covenant, a different covenant. One of the parties is God the Creator of the universe. The other party is us. God has given his blood to sign the covenant. Through Christ, God calls all humanity to a covenant or contract with Him. God did the hard part. Our part in the contract/covenant is to accept free salvation. It's just to believe in God. What a deal!

When we celebrate Holy Communion, we remember the moment in which Christ committed to this covenant – when he spilled his blood to provide salvation for us. In this special moment, we remember too that we are God's people. Through this covenant, we have salvation from sin and eternal death. It's a covenant that gives us life, joy and hope. The beautiful thing is that our part of the covenant was fulfilled by Christ on the cross.

**Examine yourself:** Am I enjoying of the benefits of this covenant that I made with God?

**Pray:** Thank you, my God, for all that you have done for me. Thank you for taking my place on the cross.

# Luke 22:31-71

*"Simon, Satan has asked to sift all of you as wheat. But I have prayed for you, Simon, that your faith may not fail. And when you have turned back, strengthen your brothers." Lk 22:31-32*

Where do the tests come from that endanger the faithfulness of the Christian? Some come from the circumstances that surround us. There are others whose author is the devil. The good news is that the devil doesn't have power over the Christian's life. However, in occasions like in this passage, God allows Satan to test us.

Jesus Christ was also tested. He was tested as a man in his obedience to his Father until his death, and also as God in the depth of his love for humanity. Therefore, we should not fear tests. Faith in God and in his promises helps us to pass these tests. Tests strengthen us in our faith. God can use us better when our life in Him is firmer and stronger, which comes from tests. Simon Peter, after passing the test, could give encouragement to his brothers in Christ who were being tested (1 Peter 4:12, 13).

**Examine yourself:** How can I make something useful from these tests that will help my spiritual growth?

**Pray:** Lord, please strengthen my faith so that I don't weaken amid the tests I face.

# Luke 23:1-56 `Day 30`

*"Father, forgive them, for they do not know
what they are doing." Luke 23:34*

The angry crowd against Jesus knew that He was not a criminal, but they ignored the fact that He was God's Son. They all screamed without thinking of the injustice that they were participating in. How different was Jesus' attitude! How would I react in such horrible moments of my life? How would I react in front of people who mercilessly hit me? How would I react when I was feeling defeated? Jesus reacted by giving back love and forgiveness. Even in the hardest situations, Jesus never stopped loving. "It (love) always protects, always trusts, always hopes, always perseveres. Love never fails." (1Corinthians 13:7-8).

Perhaps none of us faces a furious multitude, but yes, we face situations and people where we can lose control. It's in those moments when we can see how full our heart is of God's love.

**Examine yourself:** Is there some situation or person that has infuriated me this week? Has the love of God been seen in me as I dealt with that situation?

**Pray:** Lord, please give me more and more of your love, so that it is seen in me, even in my hardest moments.

# Luke 24 :1-53 `Day 31`

*"Why do you look for the living among the dead?" Luke 24:5*

"And if Christ has not been raised, our preaching is useless and so is your faith." (1 Corinthians 15:14). If Christ didn't live again, then it is a waste of time to serve him or believe in him or speak of him to others. When Christ was resurrected, He validated Christianity, "was appointed the Son of God in power" (Romans 1:4). Jesus was resurrected in body and spirit, and equally all the children of God will be resurrected. His resurrection guarantees us that we also will be resurrected with him (John 6:40).

Jesus was on several occasions with his disciples, and then he ascended to heaven. After that, Jesus' disciples dedicated themselves to telling everyone what they had seen. That is how the message came to us. Thanks to the efforts of those men and women who passed on the Word from generation to generation, we get to meet Jesus and experience his forgiveness. There are many other people who need to hear about Jesus.

**Examine yourself:** Do I believe with all my heart that Christ was resurrected, that he is alive today, and that he is present in my life?

**Pray:** Thank you God, for all that you have done for me during this study of the book of Luke.

# HOW TO READ THE BIBLE and learn from it

### Mónica E. Mastronardi

## Why is it so important to read the Bible?

*"All Scripture is God-breathed and is useful for teaching, rebuking, correcting and training in righteousness." 2 Tim. 3:16*

For millions of Christians, the Bible is the most important book in the world. Why is it so special? Here are some reasons:

1. The Bible explains the origin of all things and the purpose of their existence.
2. The Bible shows humans the path (Jesus) which leads to a relationship with God.
3. The Bible has transformed the lives of millions of people.
4. The accuracy of the historical events narrated in the Bible has been confirmed in archaeological findings.
5. The Bibles' promises and prophecies have been fulfilled through history and in the lives of the children of God.
6. Jesus believed in the Word (the Bible), studied it, lived to fulfill it, obeyed it completely and taught it.
7. Through the Bible, God speaks to the reader in a very personal way.
8. The Bible nurtures the believer's spirit with its words.
9. The Bible shows the path to a holy life.
10. The Bible comforts in times of sorrow.
11. The Bible provides a guide in moments of decision-making.
12. The Bible shows how great God's love is towards man.

All of this and much more is what the Bible is for man. An example of how difficult it is for a person to express the value of the Bible is found in Psalms 119. This is the longest chapter in the Bible: 176 verses! It's primary objective is to demonstrate the great treasure that can be found in the Word of God for all mankind.

## The Books of the Bible and ████████ Their Main Divisions.

The Bible is a complete collection of books, a library. Its name, which comes from Greek, means "small books".

The 66 books that make up the Bible were written separately and collected into the Old Testament (39 book written before Jesus) and in the New Testament (27 books written after Jesus).

Within the 40 authors of the Bible, you can find kings, prophets, shepherds, artisans, fishermen, soldiers, poets, doctors, and many other faithful men who were inspired and guided by the Spirit of God. Between some of them, there is more than 1,500 years of difference. However the consistency and the unity among these authors, the majority of them never having met, is extraordinary. There is no other book like the Bible, which, having been inspired by God, is the only one that could really satisfy all human needs.

The books of the Bible have been divided into chapters, and each chapter into verses, for ease of study and comparison between its different parts. For example, when we say Matthew 18:27, this means the book of Matthew, chapter 18, verse 27 will be read. (See the illustrations on the next page.)

When a larger or smaller portion of a verse is cited, punctuation symbols are used to indicate the extension of the reference. These symbols are used according to the chart on the next page.

The names of the books of the Bible, as well as abbreviations that maybe used, will appear on the Table of Contents page, which you can find in the first pages of a Bible. In the beginning, it is very useful to use the contents page to locate the page number of the book you are looking for.

# Bible Reference Reading Chart

| Reference | Book | Chapter | Verses |
|-----------|------|---------|--------|
| Matt. 5:3-6 | Matthew | 5 | 3 - 6 |
| Mk. 7:3, 5 | Mark | 7 | 3 & 5 |
| Jn. 4:3s | John | 4 | 3 & following 1 verse |
| Lk. 5:9ss | Luke | 5 | 9 & following verses |
| Gen. 32:30-33:9 | Genesis | 32 | Verse 30 to Chapter 33 verse 9 |

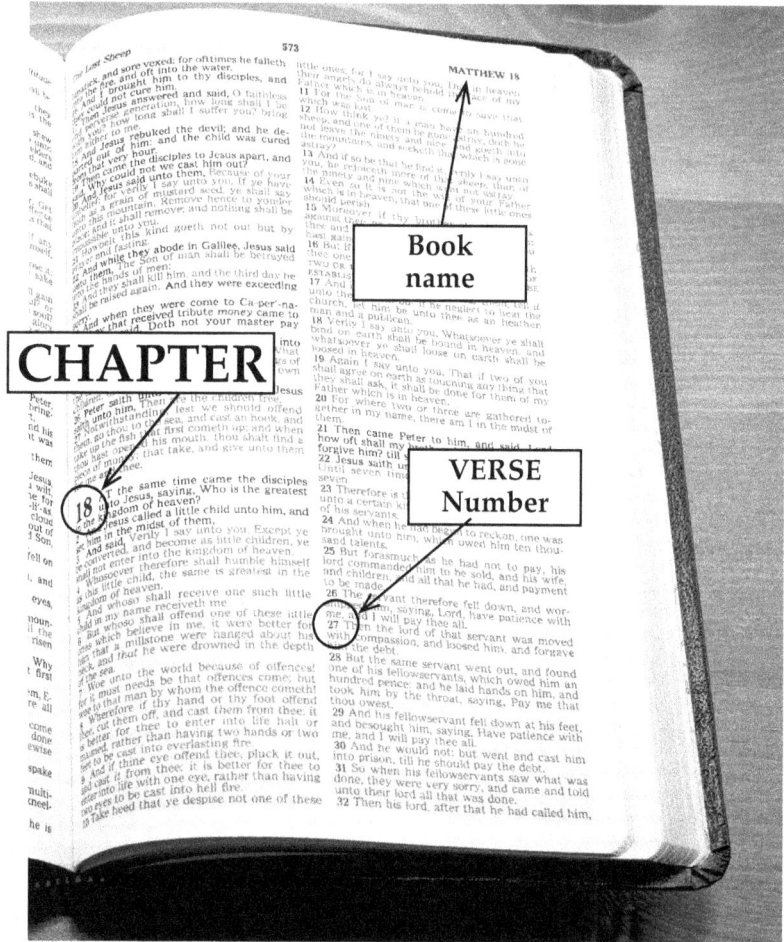

# The Bible Was Written By the Will and Mandate of God.

The first books of the Bible were written by the mandate of God to Moses. In Deuteronomy 6:6-9, it says that God told the people to spread the Word that was received through all means possible, including writing.

Moses also collected the stories of the past history of his people (Israel) in the book of Genesis.

How was Moses able to know these facts so precisely?

Archaeological discoveries have proven that since the time of Abraham (some 2000 years before Christ), there were schools that taught how to read and write. Prior to Abraham, these stories were told orally from parent to child. The Archaeological discoveries have proven that the Hebrews have known about writing since ancient times. In the book of Hebrews, 9:19, it indicates that the Israelites, from ancient times, had books where they would register everything. (See Deuteronomy 27:2-8 and Joshua 8:30-32) During those times, the writing and the materials used were very different from those used today. The Hebrew verb that translates "writing" means "splitting or sink," and it refers to the method of punching marks or wedges into clay tablets. (Wedge-like writing was the origin of the letters of the alphabet). These engravings were grouped into 600 different forms, forming different signs. Then the tablets were dried and hardened like stone, the most enduring writing material that man has ever known!

The Bible was written in three original languages:

a. Hebrew: Almost all 39 books of the Old Testament were written in this language. This Semitic language was learned by the Israelites when they came into contact with the Canaanites. By the time of Jesus, all the writings of the Old Testament had been translated to Greek.

b. Aramaic: The language learned during the Babylonian exile. Portions of Daniel and Ezra where written in it. The Old Testament books were written over a period of more than 2,000 years. The scribe Ezra worked on the compilation of these books (457 B.C.), and this was completed by the high priest Simon the Just (300 B.C.).

Aramaic became the popular language used and it was spoken by Jesus. Matthew writes his gospel in Aramaic even though it was translated into Greek.

c. Greek: This was the common language used in the Roman Empire. The books of the New Testament were written in Greek.

The authors of the New Testament also received God's command to write down the things they had witnessed. An example of this is found in Revelations 1:19, "Write, therefore, what you have seen, what is now and what will take place later."

Today, very few people read the Bible in its original languages. Thank God that the Bible has been translated into hundreds of languages commonly used today.

These translations of the Bible are called versions. The most common English versions are the New International Version (NIV), the King James Version (KJV), the New King James Version (NKJV).

# Can Such an Old Book Be a Secure Guide for Christians of the 21st Century?

*"We also have the prophetic message as something completely reliable, and you will do well to pay attention to it, as to a light shining in a dark place, until the day dawns and the morning star rises in your hearts." 2 Peter 1:19,21*

The Apostle Paul states that all men and women can find a secure guide for their life in the Word of God, continually comparing the Word of God with a lamp that lights the path, even in the thickest darkness. The Bible has this purpose until the day the Morning Star appears, referring to the day in which Christ will come again for His people. Meanwhile, Peter teaches Christians to be alert to what the Bible teaches.

The Word of God is compared to a filter which all information that comes from the world can be filtered. When one knows the Word of God, he or she can evaluate each thing through this lens to make decisions that are aligned with God's purpose for His children.

Others compare the Word of God to a lens, which enables us to discover Satan's tricks and find a secure path. Others find it similar to a compass. Others also compare it to a lighthouse which illuminates the dark sea of the world and guides the ship of our life to the secure port of eternal life.

There is a story of a captain that steered his ship in the high seas on a very dark night. Suddenly the watcher informs him of a light that he saw on the horizon. The captain sends instructions to the origin of the light, assuming it is another ship, to move, otherwise they will crash into each other. Then a message was received from the light source, that they will not move, but that his ship should be the one to change its course. The ship was very close to the light source and if a quick decision wasn't made, a crash would be inevitable. The Captain very worriedly tries one more time to try to have the light source move by mentioning his royal rights. To his surprise, he received the following response from the light source, "No matter how many royal rights you might have, Captain, you are the one that must move because the light that you see is coming from a lighthouse."

In this same way, the Word of God is also a firm and secure guide for all of us. It should not be adapted or modified according to our convenience. The Word of God doesn't change or justify any sinful conduct. It's the Word that changes the human being to live according to the commands of the Lord.

## How Can We Be Sure That the Bible Is the Word of God?

2 Peter 1:21 declares, "For prophecy never had its origin in the human will, but prophets, though human, spoke from God as they were carried along by the Holy Spirit." (NIV) The Word of God was not brought to us by the will of man, but its origin is divine. The Holy Spirit was the one who moved the prophets, through inspiration.

***Article of Faith IV of the Church of the Nazarene declares:

"We believe in the plenary inspiration of the Holy Scriptures, by which we understand the 66 books of the Old and New Testaments, given by divine inspiration, inerrantly revealing the will of God concerning us in all things necessary to our salvation, so that whatever is not contained therein is not to be enjoined as an article of faith."

Not everyone understands inspiration in the same way. Some believe that some parts of the Bible are more inspired than others.

But to confirm that God is the author of the Bible is something totally different. The Bible doesn't contain information about man's effort to know God, like in other religions, but it is how God reveals himself to humanity through human instruments. Sergio Franco explains the intention of God for the Bible with these words: "He does not want to be a hidden or unknown being." Dr. W.T Purkiser adds, "faith is the human response to the revelation of God."

It is marvelous how the Holy Spirit worked to guide each of the writers. The Spirit gave them the capability to understand the will of God and the ability to communicate it to their contemporaries in their own words.

## How Important Were the Scriptures for Jesus?

In Matthew 5:17, Jesus declares the purpose of his arrival, "Do not think that I have come to abolish the Law or the Prophets; I have not come to abolish them but to fulfill them." What did Jesus come to fulfill? The verb that Jesus used translates to "abolish," which was used in that time to point out how a house or tent was destroyed or undone.

Jesus clearly explains that he did not come to put an end to what God had already established through the mouths of his servants since the time of Moses; but on the contrary, he declares that he came to fulfill God's promises. Fulfill in its original language means to "fill to the top." That means that Jesus' goal was to:

a. **Complete** the work that his father had assigned him which had been prophesied by his servants.

b. **Fulfill** the promise that God had made to man that he would send a savior.

c. **Fulfill** the requirements of the holy and perfect lamb, the only one that could pay the price for our salvation.

d. **Put into practice** the law: Jesus not only fulfilled the ceremonial law, such as rituals established by the law, but he also maintained the moral law becoming our perfect example.

In different opportunities, Jesus declared that what he was doing was fulfilling the Scriptures. In this way, Jesus is subject to the words written by men in the Old Testament.

The disciples didn't understand the suffering that Jesus had to go through because they didn't understand what the prophets had anticipated (Luke 24:25, 27, 44).

Is it possible that their lack of understanding was because they had not studied the scriptures carefully, so they were unable to compare the scriptures to the events in which they were living?

If Jesus had not been subjected to fulfill what was written in the Old Testament about him, he would have shattered the value of the entire Word of God.

Through his incarnation Christ reveals the importance of living according to the Word of God, which many of his contemporaries had neglected. Like Jesus, Christians should respect and summit to the Word of God.

In Matthew 5:19, Jesus affirms that it is important to obey the entire Word of God: "Therefore anyone who sets aside one of the least of these commands and teaches others accordingly will be called least in the kingdom of heaven, but whoever practices and teaches these commands will be called great in the kingdom of heaven."

Jesus understood the fundamental importance of following the commandments of the Word by living according to its teachings. The Lord applied the Word in all areas of his personal life as we can see in the following examples of Scripture:

a. In times of testing and temptation: Matthew 4:1-11.

b. In his prayers: In the prayer of John 17:8, Jesus feels pleased on how he was able to complete his responsibilities by sharing the Word and living it.

c. In training of the disciples: Luke 24:27-32

d. In preaching and personal evangelism: John 3:14-15 and Matthew 11:7-11

e. To refute wrong teachings: Matthew 22:23-33

# How to Read the Bible in Three Easy Steps

When the Lord saved you, he made you a new creature so that you can grow in a new life with God. No one can grow if they are not properly fed. All people need food to grow naturally. The Word is the daily food for every Christian. The following three simple steps will help you read the Bible each day:

## Step #1:  Prepare yourself for a special time with God!

The apostle Paul calls Timothy to be responsible in the study of the Word of God (2 Timothy 3:14-17).

The Word of God should not be read as if we were reading a newspaper or any other reading material. We should approach it with respect and expectation. Every time we open the pages of the Bible, we are opening a channel of communication with God. We should not treat it as if it were an informative book, but as a living Word that always has something new and fresh for us.

Reading of the Bible is daily food for each Christian: "Jesus answered, 'It is written: "Man shall not live on bread alone, but on every word that comes from the mouth of God' " (Matthew 4:4). However, for the Word to be effective, it must enter first through our minds by reading it.

The reading of the Bible should be the most important daily task for a Christian. You should dedicate the best of your time to it, time in which your mind can concentrate only on it without being rushed. You should choose a place where it will be quiet and comfortable, away from distractions.

The Holy Spirit is the one who makes the connection between our hearts and the Word. That is why before reading, you should pray asking the Holy Spirit for direction so that he will guide you towards the truth.

## Step #2: Savor the Word!

Simply reading the Word of God doesn't nourish the believer, but reflecting on it does. Many people know the contents of the Bible like they know a history book. However, "to savor" and "to taste" are 2 different things.

In order to read better, you should seek to understand the words. Having a dictionary on hand is very helpful. Sometimes reading the passage once or twice helps with comprehension. Reading the text in different versions can broaden the range of meaning.

On some occasions, it can be helpful to use a Bible Commentary or Biblical Dictionary. Also, you can ask a mature believer about those passages that you may find more difficult to understand.

You don't have to read long portions of a text, although it is recommended to study daily portions of the same book from beginning to the end to have a better understanding, by relating what was read with the rest of the book.

On occasion, you may stop on one verse and study it further when it speaks to you in a special way.

If you are going to start to read the Bible, it is recommended to start with the Gospels of Matthew, Mark, Luke and John. Then you can continue reading the book of Acts and other books from the New Testament.

The Word of God is a fountain of teachings. It not only shows the truth, it also convicts us of our mistakes. This truth will never contradict other passages of the Scripture. When savoring the Bible text, we learn of its great wisdom and we grow in knowledge of God. There is still one more step so that the Word can really be effective.

## Step #3: Digest the Word!

In Matthew 19:3-6, the Pharisees were accused by Jesus for reading but not applying what they read to their lives.

The Word of God not only shows us what is wrong, but also what is good in the eyes of God. The Word of God should also provoke a change in the readers' life. It becomes meat to the believer through the Holy Spirit. It is like a two-edged sword that penetrates into the deepest part of the heart where the deepest secrets and motives of the human being lay. The Bible is like the eye of God that can see the deepest part of the hearts of men and women as if they were crystal.

It motivates change, not only understanding. It purifies the soul through obedience (1 Peter 1:22-23; John 17:17). That is why a Christian who doesn't read the Word is stagnant in his spiritual life. Not only will his knowledge stop, but also his spiritual growth.

A recommendation is to keep a journal of how the Word speaks to you daily, how you put it into practice and the results you see. You can also write words, phrases and questions that you need to look up. This is a very useful way to apply the Word to your life.

## Checklist for the Daily Study of God's Word

1. My attitude as I approach the Scriptures:
   - Am I doing it hoping to meet with God?
   - Am I willing to obey God in any situation that the Word reveals to me today?
   - Have I prayed to ask for the Holy Spirit's guidance and understanding of the reading?
2. My understanding of the passage:
   - Have I read the Word with understanding?
   - Have I related what I have read in this passage to other passages I've read before?
   - Have I considered the text that surrounds the passage?
   - Do I understand what these words meant for the people in that time?
3. My obedience to the Word:
   - Have I examined myself?
   - Have I confessed the sins that the Word has exposed in my life?
   - Have I asked forgiveness for those sins?
   - Have I received personal promises from the Word?
   - Have I found a commandment that I should obey?

## Bibliography

Church of the Nazarene Manual

José Flores, El texto del Nuevo Testamento.

A.T. Robertson, Word Pictures of the N.T.,

William H Vermillion, Devotional Use of the Scriptures in the Wesleyan Movement, Wesleyan Theological Journal, Vol. 16, No.1

W. T. Purkiser, A View of the Biblical Doctrine.

# Notes:

# DICTIONARY FOR NEW BELIEVERS

### Mónica E. Mastronardi de Fernández

# A

**ADOPTION:** act of love for which God adopts the new believer as his children and makes them "co-heirs with Christ" of the blessings God has prepared for his children (John 1:12, Romans 8:16) (See also CONVERSION; TO BE BORN AGAIN).

**ADULTERY:** sexual intercourse committed by a married person, outside of marriage. In the Bible, it is sometimes used in reference to idolatry, or the act of trusting in any other god or image and putting that person in the place that only belongs to the one true God (Matthew 5:27, 28, 32).

**ADVOCATE:** name Jesus gave to the Holy Spirit (John 14:16; 15:26 and 16:7).

**ALLELUIA:** word used as an expression of joy in relation to God (Rev. 19:11).

**AMEN:** word used in the worship service to express that one agrees with what is being said, done or sung. It means literally "so be it." Prayers often end with this word (1 Chronicles 16:36; Nehemiah 8:6; Ephesians 3:21).

**ANGEL:** spiritual being that serves God. Sometimes the angels carry messages sent by God to his children (Matthew 24:31, 28:2, 5, Luke 1:18-19).

**ANOINTING WITH OIL:** a tradition that Christianity inherited from Judaism. It consists of pouring a little oil on a sick person, indicating that prayers are being prayed for healing. In Old Testament times, special people were anointed with oil, such as Kings and High Priests. Oil is a symbol of the Holy Spirit, who is the one who provides the spiritual capacity to carry out the task entrusted by God. The Spirit is also the one who operates in healing the sick in obedience to the will of God and in response to the prayers of his people (James 5:14-15). (See also DIVINE HEALING.)

**APOSTLE:** usually refers to one of the twelve men chosen by Jesus (also called disciples) to continue his ministry. Paul also considered himself an apostle (2 Peter 1:1 and Romans 1:1).

**ARTICLES OF FAITH**: the declaration of doctrines that the denomination of the Church of the Nazarene believes in and shares with others (See also MANUAL OF THE CHURCH OF THE NAZARENE).

**ATONEMENT:** Refers to fact that Christ died in the place of sinners, paying the penalty for sin that the justice of God demanded. Through His death, Jesus erased the stain of sin that separated God from mankind. Through the death of Christ, God is able to reconcile the world, and the way of finding peace with God is open to everyone (2 Corinthians 5:19, Hebrews 2:17). (See also SIN, SALVATION)

# B

**BAPTISM:** rite of initiation and symbol of entrance to the family of God (church) established by Jesus, by which the new Christian testifies of their personal decision to live a new life in Christ. The ritual consists of submerging the person briefly in water, or pouring or sprinkling water only on the head of the person (Mark 16:16, John 3:22-23 and Acts 2:38-41).

**BAPTISM WITH THE HOLY SPIRIT:** the second work of the Holy Spirit in the human heart occurring sometime after conversion, which results in purity of heart and power for service. It occurs when a person reaches the point of total consecration or surrender to God. This baptism is that which occurred in the Disciples of Christ on the day of Pentecost. Sometimes the expression "being filled with the Holy Spirit" is also used "(Matthew 3:11, Mark 1:8, Luke 3:16, John 1:33, Acts 2:1-4).

**BEATITUDE:** is the promise of happiness pronounced by God (Matthew 5:3-12).

**BIBLE:** is the book that contains the collection of 66 books, written before and after Jesus' birth by God's command to faithful people. The Bible is often referred to as "The Word of God." It is the highest authority in all things concerning

Christian doctrine and life (1 Peter 1:25).

**BIG BROTHER:** Refers to the person who helps another to know Jesus and guides them in the first steps of his Christian life.

**BLASPHEMY:** the act or offense of speaking sacrilegiously about God or sacred things; or profane talk.

**BLESS, BLESSING:** to bless is to desire or to wish for the best, to praise or give something valuable to someone as well as asking for the intervention of God on behalf of another person. To be blessed is to feel happy and satisfied (Proverbs 10:22).

**BODY OF CHRIST:** is a metaphor used in the Bible referring to the unity of all true Christians who work together and continue the work that Christ began in the world. Sometimes the body of Christ refers to the invisible church (1 Corinthians 12:27, Ephesians 4:12).

**BRIDE OF CHRIST:** a figure that refers to the Church of Christ, composed of the Christians of all ages and who will meet with Him at His second coming (Ephesians 5:23). (See CHURCH.)

**BROTHERS AND SISTERS:** Words used to address other Christians, reminding us that we are all disciples of Christ, have a common origin, and belong to the family of God.

# C

**CALL:** Personal communication of the Spirit of God to a person. God calls everyone to salvation, to sanctification and to the work of the ministry (Romans 1:1; Acts 16:10; 1 Peter 1:15; Revelations 3:20).

**CALVARY:** is the name of the mountain where Christ was crucified. It literally means "the place of the skull "(Luke 23:33).

**CARNAL, CARNALITY:** describes the way in which a person is, thinks and lives before being completely cleansed from sin. It expresses servitude to sin in different areas: physical, emotional and material. Carnality concentrates on satisfying its own selfish appetites instead of seeking first to obey the will of God (Romans 8:6-8).

**CHRIST:** See also MESSIAH.

**CHRISTIAN PERFECTION:** Also called the "life of holiness," referring to the life of the people who have been completely sanctified. In the experience of Entire Sanctification, the Holy Spirit of God purifies Christians of sinful intentions and fills them with the perfect and holy love of God. Christian perfection does not refer to being free of making mistakes, or errors, which are inherent to the human condition. It is about living to honor God and carrying out our actions, thoughts, desires and human passions according to God's will. (See also ORIGINAL SIN; HOLINESS.)

**CHURCH:** followers of the Lord Jesus Christ, seen either as a local body of believers (local church) or as the sum of believers of all nations and all ages (The universal church) (Acts 9:31; 11:26).

**CIRCUMCISION**: in the Old Testament, circumcision was done by cutting off the foreskin of male babies. It meant that this new son now belonged to the people of Israel (Jewish people). This rite was instituted by God when he made a covenant with Abraham and his descendants, as a sign of the covenant of fidelity that they made with God (Genesis 17:9-14, Jeremiah 4:4). In the New Testament, circumcision acquires a spiritual meaning, pointing to the internal sign which must distinguish all God's children, which is heart purity (Romans 2:28-29).

**COMPASSION:** Deep feeling of love and interest in meeting the needs of those people who for different reasons suffer anguish, poverty, and difficulty. It's the opposite of being indifferent to the suffering of others. In the Bible, it is also called "mercy" (Matthew 15:32). (See also NCM)

**COMMUNION:** also called the Lord's Supper. A ceremony in which believers eat a small amount of bread and grape juice in memory of what Jesus did for them on the cross. Bread represents his body and the grape juice, the blood He shed for our sins. Jesus ordered this to be carried out until the Church is reunited with him in his Second Coming (Luke 22:19). (See also SECOND COMING OF CHRIST.)

**CONDEMNATION:** is the state of a person who has rejected God and lives in sin (Romans 5:16).

**CONFESSION:** is the act of admitting verbally that we have sinned against God, or to affirm what a person believes about Christ (Romans 10:9-10, 1 John 1:9, Heb. 3:1).

**CONSECRATION**: act of dedicating something to the service of God alone, such as our lives, our time, our belongings, among others (Romans 6:13-19, 12:1).

**COUNSELOR:** can apply to the Holy Spirit as well as to people who help others by giving good advice. Counseling can be carried out by the pastor, a trained counselor or a believer with more experience in the Christian life.

**CONVERSION:** believing in the Lord Jesus Christ and sincerely repenting. Conversion is made evident in a change of attitude in people who decide to change the direction of their lives in obedience to God. In the act of conversion, God forgives the sins we have committed, which has been made possible thanks to the death of Jesus for us on the cross. The repentant person receives new life and will start to grow in the knowledge of God and service for Him (Romans 6:4, 12:2, 2 Corinthians 5:17, Ephesians 4:22-24).

**CONVICTION OF SIN:** is the result of the action of the Holy Spirit in our hearts, making us feel guilty and giving us the desire to be forgiven so that our relationship with God can be restored (John 16:8).

**CRUCIFIXION:** method of torture and death used by the Roman Empire. Jesus was crucified (Matthew 27:22-23, 27).

# D

**DAY OF REST:** the day that God established from the time of the creation to rest from weekly activities and spend time in worshiping the Lord. Before Jesus' resurrection on the first day of the week (Sunday), the Jews kept Saturday for this purpose. Christians began to keep Sunday in memory of the triumph of their Lord over death (Genesis 2:1-3).

**DAY OF THE LORD:** In the some of the Old Testament prophets and in the New Testament, it sometimes refers to the time of the first and second coming of Jesus (Acts 2:20).

**DEACON / DEACONESS:** name designating a believer who has been "ordained". In other words they have received an official license or credential from the Church for some specialized service or ministry according to their gifts. The Church of the Nazarene also ordains Ministers. (See also ORDAINED MINISTERS.)

**Dedication of children:** is a ceremony performed in the presence of the congregation, where parents present their child to God and commit to educate him or her in the Word of God. The congregation also commits to help the parents in this purpose, and the pastor prays asking the blessing of God for the life of the child and his family.

**DEITY:** a term that refers to God, as the Trinity (Father, Son and Holy Spirit). It is used to affirm that Jesus Christ is God (Colossians 2:9).

**DEVIL**: See SATAN.

**DISCIPLE:** a disciple is one who learns, guided by a teacher. The term is for all those followers of Jesus who are learning from his teachings and are applying them to their lives (Luke 6:10, 14:27).

**DISTRICT:** a set of local churches found in a particular geographic area which are under the responsibility of a District Superintendent. (See also DISTRICT SUPERINTENDENT.)

**DISTRICT ADVISORY BOARD:** body of district leaders formed by the District Superintendent, ordained ministers and lay members elected in the Annual District Assembly, by the representatives of the local churches. District Advisory Board accompanies the ministry of the District Superintendent as the leader of the local churches within their jurisdiction. (See also DISTRICT.)

**DISTRICT SUPERINTENDENT:** the leader of a jurisdiction or district of the Church of the Nazarene. This person is responsible for the pastors of local churches and leaders of the district ministries in order to advance the Kingdom of God. (See also DISTRICT.)

**DIVINE HEALING:** Physical healing that takes place miraculously in an instant or progressive way and which proceeds from the hand of God. This healing occurs in response to the faith prayer of believers and when it is the will of God (John 4:46-53).

**DOCTRINE:** It applies to the set of beliefs of Christianity (Acts 2:42).

**DYING TO SELF:** is the act of allowing Christ to have absolute control of our whole being. The Apostle Paul uses this figure of death to express that Christians must refuse to live governed by their human desires and passions, and live their lives according to the holy will of God (Romans 8:13, Colossians 3:5). See also CONSECRATION; SANCTIFIED; ENTIRE SANCTIFICATION.

# E

**ENTIRE SANCTIFICATION:** grace received from God when the believer receives by faith the fullness of the Holy Spirit, which enables him to live a life of purity. The will of God is that all His children are entirely sanctified. The Holy Spirit fills Christians when they understand that they need to surrender the control of their lives to the lordship of Christ, and refuse to live focused on their own wills. It must be distinguished from the initial sanctification that occurs when a person accepts Christ as their personal savior (2 Thessalonians 2:13). It is the distinctive doctrine of Wesleyan Arminian churches. (See also BAPTISM WITH THE HOLY SPIRIT, I (EGO).)

**ETERNAL LIFE:** the life of the Christian that continues after death (Colossians 3:1-4).

**EVANGELICALS:** The branch of the Protestant church which focuses on salvation in Christ, through grace, by faith and based only on the authority of the Scriptures.

# F

**FAITH:** This word is used in three ways: to believe in something that you cannot prove or see; the action of placing all confidence in Christ for salvation; or it can also indicate the set of the fundamental beliefs of Christianity (Hebrews 11:1,6, Matthew 17:20, Romans 1:17).

**FALL, FALLING INTO SIN:** is the act of sinning or returning to life in sin after conversion (Jeremiah 2:19, 14:7).

**FASTING:** is the voluntary abstention of food to dedicate this time to prayer and study of the Word. It is one of the spiritual disciplines which are practiced by Christians for different purposes for their spiritual growth (Matthew 4:1-2; Acts 13:2-3).

**FINAL JUDGMENT:** Future event predicted in the Bible which will consist of the judgment of all mankind before Jesus Christ, after Jesus' second coming (Matthew 25:31-46).

**FLOCK:** Used sometimes to refer to the group of faithful who are under the responsibility of a pastor. It is a figure taken from the shepherding scenes from biblical times. Frequently the Bible compares the people of Israel and the church to a flock which needs to be guided. The main function of Pastors is to ensure the welfare of their flock, giving account to God to whom the sheep belong (John 21:15-18). (See also PASTOR.)

**FORNICATION:** Refers to relationships between persons of the opposite sex outside of marriage. It can also describe metaphorically infidelity toward God (1 Corinthians 6:9).

**FRUIT OF THE SPIRIT:** Refers to the results of the work of the Holy Spirit in the life of the Christian, listed in Galatians 5:22-23.

**FULLNESS OF THE HOLY SPIRIT:** See ENTIRE SANCTIFICATION.

# G

**GENERAL SUPERINTENDENT:** The Church of the Nazarene has a General Superintendent for each one of the regions of the world, divided geographically for administrative purposes. These are elected at the General Assembly held every four years with delegates from all Districts. General Superintendents have the responsibility to ensure the unity of the church and the permanence of the church in biblically-based doctrines. They attend to administrative matters of their jurisdiction, conduct District Assemblies and carry out the ordination of Ministers.

**GIFTS:** skills or abilities received from God through the Holy Spirit to perform some Christian service. For example: teaching, provide for the needs of others, healing the sick, among others (1 Corinthians 12:4; Romans 12:6; 1 Corinthians 12:31-13:13).

**GLORIFICATION:** See RESURRECTION.

**GOOD DEEDS:** It is every action of goodness carried out by Christians to other people as evidence of their genuine love and interest in others. These good works should be normal and every day occurrences in the life of the children of God (Ephesians 2:10).

**GOSPEL:** The message of good news about the life and work of Jesus to save humanity. The first four books of the New Testament that narrate the birth, life, death and resurrection of Jesus Christ are called the Gospels (2 Timothy 1:9-10).

**GRACE:** is the love of God given freely to mankind (Ephesians 2:4-10).

**GREAT COMMISSION:** the last instructions that Jesus gave to his disciples before ascending to heaven (Matthew 28:18-20).

**GREAT COMMANDMENT:** Summary made by Jesus of all that God expects of His children, recorded in Matthew 22:36-39.

# H

**HEART:** is the organ of the human body that in the Bible is used as a synonym for all that which makes us humans, such as feelings, motivations, desires and the will. In the heart can also be found moral qualities that guide the behavior of each person (Ephesians 3:17, Romans 10:10, Mark 10:30).

**HELL:** In Hebrew "hades", a place of eternal existence and punishment where those who have rejected Christ go after judgment. (Luke 16:23, Matthew 13:41-43).

**HOLINESS:** is the very essence of God, who is without sin. In the Old Testament, this term is applied to any person or object that was consecrated to the service of God. In the New Testament, it applies to Jesus and the members of his church. Holiness is a mandate of God for all His Children so that they may live far away from sin. It involves being cleansed of original sin, and in loving God and our neighbors with all our hearts (1 Thessalonians 4:3-7). (See also SANCTIFIED, ENTIRE SANCTIFICATION.)

**HOLY SPIRIT:** He is the third Person of the Trinity through whom God works in this world (John 14:26).

**HOLY WEEK:** week in which we commemorate the events that took place during the crucifixion, death and resurrection of the Lord Jesus Christ. The week begins with Palm Sunday and ends on Easter Day or Sunday of Resurrection.

**HOSANNA:** Literally "save, I pray", used to invoke the blessing of God, through Jesus Christ (the Messiah) (Mark 11:9-10).

**HYMNBOOK:** Book used in Christian churches containing songs of praise that declare the greatness and wonders of the Lord.

# I

**INNATE SIN:** See ORIGINAL SIN

**INTERCESSION:** is the action of intervening on behalf of another. Jesus is the supreme example as the mediator between God and mankind as a divine priest provided by God in order to restore the relationships broken by sin. An intercessor is also a Christian who prays to God for the needs of other people (Hebrews 9:14-15, John 17). See also PRAYER.

# J

**JEHOVAH:** word used to refer to the only true God, used in the times of the Old Testament; word from the Hebrew language (Exodus 3:15).

**JOY:** deep experience of immense happiness which is the fruit of the work of the Holy Spirit in the life of the believer. Not to be confused with the happy feelings depending on one's mood. This "joy" remains in the believer's heart despite the difficulties they may face in this life (Luke 2:10, John 15:11).

**JUSTIFICATION:** term used by the apostle Paul to express the forgiving grace of God to the repentant sinner and makes him "righteous" before God, declaring Him free from guilt and worthy of communion with his Creator (Romans 4:25 and 5:18).

**JUSTIFIED:** someone who has been made righteous or declared righteous by God (Romans 5:1).

# K

**KINDNESS:** is a voluntary and disinterested act whose objective is to satisfy the need of another person.

**KING OF KINGS:** one of the titles of Christ, referring to His unlimited authority and power over and above any other authority that may exist in the universe. As King of Kings, He will judge all the leaders of the nations as to whether they have fulfilled their responsibilities. The Bible teaches that all authority is derived from divine authority and that in the final judgment, all people in government functions will be judged by Christ according to the laws and principles of the Kingdom of God (Revelations 17:14). (See also KINGDOM OF GOD; SECOND COMING OF CHRIST.)

**KINGDOM OF GOD:** the government of Christ and His unlimited authority. God's kingdom must be understood in its three historical times: a) The kingdom came with Christ, for He is the king of the God's Kingdom; b) The Kingdom is expanding currently within each new person who accepts the lordship of Christ for his life; c) The Kingdom will come to full fruition at the second coming of Christ when He will have unlimited and eternal dominion over His people and the universe (Mark 1:14-15). (See also KING OF KINGS.)

# L

**LAITY:** Every believer in a local church, excluding ordained ministers. (See MINISTER; MINISTRY; DEACON, MINISTER.)

**LAMB OF GOD:** figure that points to Christ as the sacrifice provided by God once and forever on the cross. He came to replace the many animals that were sacrificed annually by the Jewish people to obtain forgiveness from God for their sins. These animal sacrifices without defect were to remind the people that God would send the Messiah, the perfect lamb (without sin) as an offering of sacrifice in for the sins of mankind (John 1:36).

**LOCAL CHURCH BOARD:** is the body of leaders of a church composed of members elected at the annual church meeting. This board assists the pastor, ensuring good planning, administration and the expansion of ministries and properties of the local church.

**LORD:** Title frequently used in the New Testament to mark Christ as master and owner of the life of the Christian and His church. In the Old Testament, the term also applies to God the Father (Matthew 11:25).

**LORD OF LORDS:** See KING OF KINGS.

**LORDSHIP OF CHRIST:** See LORD.

**LORD'S SUPPER:** SEE COMMUNION.

**LORD'S DAY:** Sunday which is the day when Christians gather to worship the Lord Jesus Christ (Revelation 1:10).

# M

**MANUAL OF THE CHURCH OF THE NAZARENE:** a book containing a historical summary of the origin of the name of the church, the organizational and governance procedures, and how Nazarenes should behave in the face of contemporary problems such as, abortion; euthanasia; homosexuality and others.

**MEMBER:** refers to a believer who has accepted to be part of the official list of members of a local church. It is taken from the Biblical figure of the Body of Christ, of which all true Christians are members. Participation as an active member of a local church allows the Christian certain benefits and also gives the believer responsibilities in ministry. Jesus taught his disciples that they should remain united in order to make an effective impact on this world (John 17:11; Romans 12:4-5; 1 Corinthians 12:12-13).

**MERCY:** is an act of grace, love and God's own compassion and imparted to his children by the Holy Spirit. This feeling is not an end in itself, but its purpose is to mobilize Christians to reach out to the needy in the same way that God has been merciful to us all (Matthew 5:7). (See also COMPASSION.)

**MESSIAH:** Hebrew word meaning "the anointed one", the title given to the Savior promised by God to the people in the Old Testament. Messiah in Greek is "Christ". (See REDEMPTION.)

**MINISTER, MINISTRY:** A minister is usually a person called by God to serve in the church. The term Minister is used to designate those in leadership, principally the clergy as the pastors. Although in the Bible the use of the term is more comprehensive, including all those who serve the purposes of God with their lives. Nowadays, some churches have several ministers such as youth pastor, Sunday school ministries pastor, minister of compassion, leader of the music ministry, among others. Ministry includes everything that is done to serve God. Ministry can be applied to different areas of service such as the ministry of preaching, the worship ministry, among others (Acts 20:24; Colossians 1:7).

**MIRACLE:** supernatural deed done by the power of God. They are also called "wonders" or "signs."

**MISSIONARY:** is a person called by God to dedicate his/her life full-time being sent by the church with a special mission to another geographical region, social group or a different culture. In a broader sense, the term applies to any person who overcomes obstacles presenting the message of salvation and bringing people to Jesus, making disciples and training others for Christian leadership. The Church of the Nazarene recognizes the people who are called by God to missionary work and sends them to other countries to help in the extension and consolidation of churches. These missionaries are sustained by the prayers and offerings from local churches, and their work is coordinated by the International Board of World Mission (Acts 1:8).

# N

**NAZARENE:** word designating all the citizens of Nazareth during the time of Jesus. It was a little town of the Jewish district of Galilee. The name of the Church of the Nazarene derives its name from this fact, because Jesus was a Nazarene (Matthew 2:23).

**NAZARENE MISSIONS INTERNATIONAL (NMI):** a supporting church department which promotes and supports the missions work of the Church of the Nazarene throughout the world.

**NAZARENE YOUTH INTERNATIONAL (NY):** is the ministry of the Church of the Nazarene that works specifically with young people (twelve years and over) to bring them to the new life in Christ and make them His disciples.

**NEW TESTAMENT (N.T.):** The set of 27 books of the Bible that were written after death of Jesus. These tell the life of Christ and the beginnings of the Christian church.

**NCM:** Acronym of Nazarene Compassionate Ministries. See also COMPASSION

**OLD TESTAMENT (O.T.):** is the name for the set of 39 books of the Bible that were written before the birth of Jesus.

**OFFERINGS:** all that we present to God as an act of worship. In the churches, Christians are accustomed to giving offerings, which are voluntary contributions, during worship services and meetings. These, together with tithes, are used to support the ministries and properties of the church. There are other special offerings that are regularly raised in the Churches of the Nazarene throughout the world to contribute to World Missions:

- **Alabaster Offering:** Collected in September and in February. It is used in the construction of buildings and the purchase of land for hospitals, seminaries, schools, churches and Pastors' houses.

- **Thanksgiving Offering:** Collected in November and is used for World Evangelism.

- **World Mission Broadcast Offering:** Collected in June and used for the radio programs of the Church of the Nazarene in missionary areas.

- **Easter Offering:** This offering is collected on Easter Sunday and is used for World Evangelism.

- **Medical Plan Offering:** Collected in the month of May, used to defray medical expenses of active and retired missionaries.

- **Compassionate Ministries Offering:** Collected in the month of December for the projects of Compassionate Ministries and used to provide assistance in catastrophic situations and natural disasters.

- **Prayer and Fasting Offering:** Collected in all months of the year, the purpose is to promote prayer, fasting and the self-sacrificing offering in favor of World Evangelism. (See also FASTING.)

**ORDAINED MINISTER:** is the minister that the Church has ordained (officially recognized as being qualified and prepared to officially be a pastor). Among the requirements to be considered as a candidate for this title are: theological studies, ministerial experience, and personal testimony and

Christian service, among others.

**ORIGINAL SIN:** a human condition inherited and shared by the whole human race which imprints in our hearts rebellion against God's will and encourages us to live following our own desires and whims. The Sacrifice of Christ on the cross makes it possible for this condition to be cleansed from the human heart in order to free us to obey God. This happens when we recognize that there is selfishness in our hearts, and that this prevents us from fulfilling God's perfect will in all the spheres of our life, and when we sincerely wish to be free from this bondage. This work of the Holy Spirit is known as; 'Sanctification',' Christian Perfection', 'Baptism of the Spirit' or being filled with the Spirit. While original sin has not been cleansed, the Holy Spirit cannot completely fill our hearts and we will always have trouble obeying the will of God for our lives (Ephesians 2:3). (See BAPTISM WITH THE HOLY SPIRIT.)

# P

**PASTOR:** Christian leader of a local church called by God to guide the believers and lead them in the fulfillment of God's purposes for His people (Acts 20:28). (See also FLOCK.)

**PENTECOST:** Jewish feast celebrated 50 days after Easter. It was during the Feast of Pentecost that the disciples of Jesus assembled after Jesus' ascension to heaven. They were filled with the Holy Spirit and began to preach for the first time to a great multitude who had gathered in the city of Jerusalem for the feast. On this occasion, the disciples experienced a miracle of the Holy Spirit that enabled them to preach in the different dialect languages of the listeners. As a result, about three thousand people became Christians that day. Pentecost was the day that the church was born (Acts 2:1-42).

**PERFECT LOVE:** is the experience of loving God with all one's heart, soul, mind and strength. To love God above all things and to live constantly fulfilling his will (Matthew 27:38-19).

**PRAISE:** is worship expressed in words or songs that exalt the greatness and generous acts of our God. (Isaiah 25:1).

**PRAYER:** dialogue with God which allows us to maintain an intimate relationship daily with Him.

**PROFESSION OF FAITH:** Public demonstration that people make claiming that they believe in Christ as their only Savior and that from now on they will submit their lives to the Lordship of Christ. (See also CONVERSION.)

**PROPHET:** in the Old Testament, prophets were people chosen by God to convey His Word to the nation. These messages had two main purposes:1) Telling the people that they had sinned, and call them to repentance. 2) To make known to the faithful the events that would occur at a future time. These events were related to God's plan for the salvation of mankind (prophecy). In the New Testament, "prophet" is sometimes used instead of "preacher" (Ephesians 4:11; Jonah 1:1-2).

**PROPITIATION:** to propitiate, to atone for. Jesus died on the cross in our place, taking on himself the wrath of God that we deserved. This act made possible the reconciliation between mankind and God. This generous surrender of Christ, putting his life in the place that we humans deserved, makes possible the reconciliation of every sinner with his Creator (John 3:16).

**PROTESTANTS:** a movement of Christians who in the Sixteenth-century, reformed and broke away from the Roman Catholic Church. Protestants have in common some fundamentals such as: a) The Bible is the only source of authority for the Christian life. b) Each individual has the right to address God without the need of a mediator or the need to confess sins to a Priest; c) The forgiveness of sins or justification is obtained only by faith in the sacrifice of Christ. Personal sacrifices and good works are not sufficient or valid to obtain divine forgiveness; d) Christ is the head of the church and the Church is everywhere where there is a group of Christians; e) Every believer has gifts and responsibilities in Christian ministry, both ordained ministers, as well as lay people; and f) There are only two sacraments Baptism and the Lord's Supper, which were ordained by Christ.

# R

**RECONCILIATION:** Term used to describe the restoration of broken relationships between humans and God as the consequence of sin. The initiative for reconciliation comes from God and was carried out when He sent His Son as an intermediary. The children of God have the responsibility to continue this ministry of reconciliation so that many people have the opportunity to enjoy a loving relationship with their Creator. In this, Christians are "ambassadors" sent by God as his representatives to every man, woman and child to bring them back to having peace with God (Romans 5:10; Matthew 5:24; 2 Corinthians 5:18).

**REDEMPTION, REDEEMER:** The word 'redeem' means "to buy back." The term was used specifically in reference to the purchase of a slave's freedom. Jesus on the cross gave full payment, to buy our freedom from the domain of Sin when he died on our behalf (Mark 10:45; Romans 3:23-24; Ephesians 1:7). See also MESSIAH.

**REGENERATION:** is the way the Spirit of God gives new spiritual life to the person who accepts Christ as their personal Savior. Regenerate implies being born anew (John 3:33). (See also BORN AGAIN.)

**RESURRECTION:** when someone who was dead comes back to life. The Bible tells us of some people who God raised from the dead, but they all died again later like all human beings. The only one who rose again for everlasting life was Jesus. His resurrection is proof that God will keep His promise to all His children; they will be raised in the second coming of Christ and will live eternally with Him. God will work this transformation in his Children, giving them eternal and immortal bodies. This is called "glorification" (Matthew 28:1-10; Acts 2:31; John 5:25).

**RESTITUTION:** indicates the correction of an evil that has been done. It is the natural consequence of genuine repentance. An example of restitution can be seen in the life of Zacchaeus (Luke 19:1-10).

**REVIVAL:** times of Spiritual Awakening which the Holy Spirit brings to the church, characterized by a deep desire in believers to live holy lives, and to engage in evangelism, education and service ministries, resulting in many people repenting and giving their lives to the Lord.

**SACRAMENT:** It is the outward sign of grace (gift) received from God, which is expressed in a sacred ordinance or rite in which we participate. The two sacraments instituted by Christ and practiced by the Church of the Nazarene are Baptism and Holy Communion (Matthew 28:19; 26:26-29). (See also BAPTISM, COMMUNION, GRACE.)

**SALVATION:** refers to the act of Jesus Christ of dying on the cross and giving His life as a sacrifice for the forgiveness of the sin of all humanity. By means of salvation, every person can be released from the guilt of sin and the sentence of eternal death if they believe in Jesus Christ, and accept to be His disciple and continue to grow in the Christian life (Luke 2:10-11, Matthew 1:21, Corinthians 15:21, 28; 1 Peter 2:2). (See also REDEMPTION.)

**SANCTIFIED:** a person who has been filled with the Holy Spirit (Romans 8:1-2).

**SATAN:** an evil angel, spiritual enemy of God and his children. He is also called "the devil" and the "Prince of this world." He exists to incite people to rebel against God's purposes. Christ came to end his dominion and offer the only way for people to leave the slavery to which that Satan has subjected them. His defeat will be finally accomplished at the second coming of Christ, when Satan will lose all power to act in this world and its inhabitants (1 John 3:8, John 12:31, Matthew 25:41; Luke 10:19).

**SAVIOR:** see REDEEMER.

**SECOND COMING OF CHRIST:** future event that will occur at the end of earthly time when Christ will return and begin a succession of events such as: a) The resurrection of the dead; b) The marriage of the lamb, where Christ will meet with His church to celebrate together; c) The final judgment, where Christ will decide the eternal destiny of every person; d) The final battle between the army of God and the followers of Satan; e) The casting of Satan, the demons and all sinners into the eternal lake of fire; f) The restoration of the universe and the earth from all the consequences of sin and; g) The descent of the Heavenly City, the New Jerusalem and the establishment of the eternal Kingdom of God, where Christ will reign forever over his people (Revelation 19:9; 20:1-3; 21:1-10; 22:1-5).

**SELF (EGO):** the human will, mind and flesh that seek to satisfy their own desires instead of satisfying the will of God. This can be seen when believers wish to break with sinful habits of their old lives. They find themselves in a struggle between their old life and their life in Christ. This causes sadness, because they desire to do what they want to, but they can't seem to. The way out of this spiritual conflict is to hand over these selfish desires to the Lordship of Christ so that He may take control over all areas of their lives, which we call Consecration. Then the Holy Spirit will fill them and cleanse the "ego" out of their hearts, enabling them to live in harmony. (See SANCTIFIED, ENTIRE SANCTIFICATION, ORIGINAL SIN, DYING TO SELF.)

**SEMINARIES:** study centers and schools where biblical and ministerial programs are given to train Christian leaders.

**SIN:** is to disobey and rebel against the known will of God. Sins can be a bad thought, rejecting God, idolizing oneself, being selfish, and trusting oneself and our own human efforts, doing things that displease God, refusing to obey God's specific instructions, etc. It literally means "to miss the mark." People who commit sin must confess their sin in the presence of God and of the person offended (if it is a personal offense) and seek immediately divine forgiveness. Moreover, Jesus taught that the fault should be corrected and abandoned. The death of Christ on the cross is what makes it possible for Individual sin to be forgiven by God when there is sincere repentance. The Bible distinguishes two kinds of sin: innate/original/ inherited sin; and secondly, "sins of action", in other words, actions and thoughts committed in contradiction to the divine will (John 15:4; 12:14). (See also ORIGINAL SIN.)

**SLANDER:** is denigrating, belittling people with the intention of discrediting them (Proverbs 25:23).

**SPIRITUAL GROWTH:** signals the continuous and normal development of a Christian towards maturity. For this growth to occur, Christians must practice the spiritual disciplines (To learn correctly from the Word, relate to God through prayer, among others) as well as share in the fellowship of the church (2 Peter 3:18).

**STEWARDSHIP:** recognizes that God is the owner of our life and of everything we possess, so that people are only administrators of all the things received from God. Christians recognize Christ as their Lord, and understand that they must serve Him with all they are and all that has been given to them. Jesus wants His disciples to be good stewards at work managing all areas of their lives according to the will of God; for example, our gifts and talents, time, family, service, and material possessions, among others (1 Peter 4:10).

**STEWARD:** a member of the Church of the Nazarene who is chosen for responsibilities such as visitation, finance, evangelism, compassion, public worship, discipleship, preparation and the distribution of the elements for the Lord's supper, among others.

**SUNDAY SCHOOL:** A ministry of the church which organizes and promotes the teaching of the Word of God. It is called Sunday School due to the fact that on Sundays, people are grouped according to their ages in classes for the systematic study of the Word of God under the guidance of a Christian teacher. (See also SUNDAY SCHOOL MINISTRIES.)

**SUNDAY SCHOOL AND DISCIPLESHIP MINISTRIES (SDMI):** one of the ministries of the Church of the Nazarene. Its main objective is to make Christlike disciples by teaching Christians of all ages to study the Word of God and help them apply the teachings to their daily lives. This ministry coordinates and plans different programs and activities such as Sunday School; Vacation Bible School; Camps; Children's Church; Women`s Ministries; Men's Ministries; Ministry to senior citizens as well as Ministries with married couples and families. (See also SUNDAY SCHOOL.)

# T

**TALENT:** currency that was used in the time of Jesus. He used it to illustrate responsibility and fidelity that everyone has to be a good administrator of what they have received from the Creator (Matt. 25:14-30).

**TEMPLE, SANCTUARY:** building or meeting place for Christians to worship God and receive instruction from the Bible. The Bible also refers to the Christian's body as the Temple of the Holy Spirit (1 Corinthians 3:16-17; 2 Corinthians 6:16).

**TEMPTATION:** incitement to do evil (sin) which may come from Satan, from other people, or from one's selfish desires or of the bad habits acquired (James 1:12).

**TESTIMONY:** sharing with others about one's relationship with Jesus and the benefits received from this relationship. The Christian's testimony is the most effective tool for evangelism. Jesus said that all his disciples should be his "witnesses." Christians also testify to other Christians about the blessings received from God to encourage one another and mutually stimulate growth in the Christian life (Acts 2:32).

**TESTS AND TRIALS:** Difficult situations that come to the life of the Christian. These contribute to the believer's growth, providing the opportunity to test the Lord's faithfulness as well as their own commitment to Jesus Christ (1Peter 4:12-13).

**THE LORD'S SUPPER:** See COMMUNION.

**THEOLOGICAL TRAINING FOR MINISTRY:** carried out by leaders of districts and theological institutions with the objective of training people who have been called by God to leadership in the church.

**THEOLOGY:** is the science that has the object of studying, understanding and teaching about God and about His relationship with mankind.

**TITHES:** represents a tenth of all the income of a person or a family. The tithes, from the Old Testament times, were an offering of gratitude to support the priests. We understand that everything we have belongs to the Lord (for we receive everything from Him). In this act of worship, we recognize that God is owner and Lord of all we possess. The faithfulness of Christians who put aside their tithe brings great blessing to their lives, families and the people of God. It also provides the necessary funds to support the minister and the different ministries of the church (Malachi 3:10).

**TO BE BORN AGAIN:** people are born again when they repent or experience the forgiveness of their sin and begin a new life guided by God (John 3:5-8.) (See also CONVERSION.)

**TRINITY:** name that describes the union of the three Persons of God: Father, Son and Holy Spirit. The three Persons remain in a perfect relationship and participate in the holy plan of God to rescue people from sin and restore them to perfect communion with God.

# U

**USHER:** person who performs a specific service in the church such as distributing bulletins, carrying messages in an Assembly, as well as welcoming people, among others.

# V

**VIRGIN BIRTH:** refers to conception and birth of Jesus by his mother Mary. Jesus was miraculously conceived by the Holy Spirit in Mary, a young servant of God who had not had sexual relations with anyone. She was engaged to be married to Joseph, who would later become Jesus' earthly father commissioned by God to take care of the child and his mother (Luke 1:26-38; Matthew 1:18-21).

# W

**WORSHIP:** worship is profound love that springs naturally from the heart of Christians in response to the love of God that they have experienced in their hearts. This feeling gives honor and glory to the Lord as the sovereign of their lives and of the whole of creation. Worship is the voluntary act of the believer through which he expresses his love for God. (Matthew 4:10).

# Notes:

# Keys to an Abundant Christian Life
**Additional Resources**

## Level B2 – From Baptism to Membership

# WHAT WE BELIEVE AS NAZARENES

## Mónica E. Mastronardi de Fernández

## Introduction

Now days, people are bombarded through media, literature, music, and education with ideas such as:

1.  "Don't let anyone tell you what you can or cannot do," or in other words, Don't let God tell you how you must live.

2.  "It is good to believe in some God if that faith helps you be a successful person." That is equivalent to saying, Choose a god in your image and likeness and make it your servant.

3.  "All that you have, and all that you have become in life, is due to your own efforts and personal talent," or, You have received nothing from God, therefore you owe him nothing, so you don't need him in your life.

4.  "The important thing is that you feel good." In other words, Your feelings are your god. Live to satisfy them and you'll be happy.

In reality, there isn't anything new in these ideas. Their origins go back to the Garden of Eden. Satan tempted Eve through the serpent with the same invitation: Indulge your whims and desires; do your own thing. Ignore the will of the Creator and nothing bad will happen! (Genesis 3:1-6.).

From that time to now, there have been those who prefer to build a god to suit their preferences instead of building their lives in obedience to the perfect will of God, revealed in His Son Jesus Christ and His Word (1 Tim.3:9).

The Christian Church, from its origins, has combated misleading ideas like these that tried to infiltrate congregations, by constant and responsible teaching of the truth revealed by God and healthy doctrine (Titus 1:1; 2 Timothy. 4:1-5).

Over time, it became more and more necessary in the history of the church to make lists of core beliefs or "creeds" to counteract teachings contrary to the Word of God.

The Church of the Nazarene, like other Christian churches, has compiled a list of the basic biblical doctrines or articles of faith that summarize and present the main teachings of the Word in an orderly manner. These doctrines help us more easily identify those beliefs that have no foundation in the truth revealed in the Bible.

It is hoped that those who are going to be received as members in the Church of the Nazarene will publicly confess before the congregation that they accept these Articles of Faith, and will strive to live according to their teaching.

For the Church of the Nazarene, it's very important to teach our members to live according to the will of God. Being a disciple of Christ is not just about changing your mind about some things, but about living a new life. Gradually, the Christian discovers that all things are made new in his life through his study of the Word, prayer, teachings received in the local church, and the work of the Holy Spirit in his life. As your understanding of Scripture increases, you will see that God's Word is alive, powerfully transforming your whole being. As a result, you will discover that you have new goals and new attitudes. You think differently. You have new feelings. You start doing things that you didn't previously do, and you avoid some things that you used to do.

In this book, you will find the 16 Articles of Faith as they appear in the Manual of the Church of the Nazarene. Each will be followed by explanations with biblical references and applications for the believer's life and ministry in the local church.

# I. THE TRIUNE GOD

**We believe** *in one eternally existent, infinite God, Sovereign Creator and Sustainer of the universe; that He only is God, holy in nature, attributes, and purpose. The God who is holy love and light is Triune in essential being, revealed as Father, Son, and Holy Spirit.*

## 1. God is one.

The Bible reveals the existence of the one true God, and condemns every attempt by mankind to lift up any created thing as their God.[1]

Since there is only one God, he who puts his life and destiny in the hands of man-made gods deceives himself (Deuteronomy 32:37-38; Isaiah 45:20; Jer. 10:5.). This god may be yourself, another human being alive or dead (Acts 14:8-14), an animal or plant or something in the cosmos (Deuteronomy 4:19.), a spiritual being (angel or demon) or an image that represents them (Jer. 16:20; 1 Cor. 10:20; Rev. 22:8-9).

Regardless of who or what that god is, or how miraculous or powerful it seems to be or capable of giving to those who believe in it, it can never match the one true God.

All of these "gods" don't deserve to be called "God", because they are gods only for those who believe that they are (Isaiah 46:2-7; Hosea 9:10). In the Bible, they are called "idols", "images", "other gods", "gods". Believing in them is idolatry, and whoever does it is called an idolater.

Other forms of idolatry are also condemned, such as covetousness (Ephesians 5:5.), consulting fortune tellers or witches (2 Chronicles 33:6; Nahum 3:4), horoscopes (Jeremiah 10:2-3), vanity (Jeremiah 18:15), and prayer, sacrifices and hymns directed to images (Isaiah 44:17; Hosea 14:3).

Hence the importance of this first article is that it describes the only one who is truly God, who, unlike the false gods mentioned, is eternal, infinite, holy, sovereign, creator and sustainer of His creation, the origin and final destiny of everything that exists.

## 2. God is eternal and infinite.

Eternal means that His existence has no beginning or end. Also, He is infinite, that is He is always present in every place in the universe (Jer. 23:23-24). This is because God is Spirit, that is, he does not have a material body (Jn. 4:24). That is why the Word affirms that God is always with his children (Psalms 139:7).

## 3. God is Creator, Ruler, and Sustainer of the universe.

In His Word, God is revealed as the owner and Lord of all that exists (Dt. 6:4-5). This is His right as creator and sustainer of life (Gen. 1).

All of creation has come to exist through His will and is for the completion of His holy purposes. He has created the natural cycles that maintain the order of creation, such as gravity, photosynthesis (the transformation of carbon dioxide into oxygen by plants), the cycle of water purification (evaporation, condensation and rain), the rotation of the moon that regulates the oceans and seas, the regular circuits of the winds, among others.

God is not only the originator of life, but also is the one who makes life continue, sustaining it by His power. It can be said that just as an automobile depends on fuel to run, in the same way the universe depends on God in order to continue existing.

## 4. God is holy in nature, attributes, and purpose.

The Word affirms that God is holy, and this holiness is not just one more of his qualities, but constitutes His essential character. (Lev. 19:2; Ex. 15:1; Psalms 22:3; John 17:11). This means that we can call Him Holy, in the same manner that we call Him God, because "Holy is His name" (Isaiah 57:15; Lev. 1:49). What does the Bible mean when it affirms that God is holy?

a. In the first place, to say that God is holy expresses the idea that He is "separated or apart", or that he is elevated over His creation as ruler in majesty and glory. His presence exudes power, holiness and noble majesty that provokes reverent fear in mankind.

The Old Testament gives the testimonies of Isaiah and Moses who were permitted to see from afar the glory of God. The first reaction of the prophet Isaiah before the magnificence and noble presence of the Lord was of terror. "Woe is me, I am a dead man" he exclaimed when he felt unworthy to be face to face before the holiness of the Creator (Isaiah 6:3-5). Moises worshiped Him after being in His presence saying, "Who is like You, oh Jehovah, among the gods? Who is like you, glorious in holiness?" (Ex. 15:11).

Reverence and respect for God must be the constant attitude of the believer, and even more when entering into the presence of God through prayer, when entering worship, when praising His name and learning His Word. God is the holy ruler of each moment of your life.

b.  Secondly, the Bible describes His purity, perfection, and perfect righteousness. God is pure in His intentions and every decision. His plan for humanity is perfect. Holiness is the opposite of evil. Because God is holy, he does not tolerate evil, and nothing contaminated with sin can be in relation with Him or be close to Him. That is why when Adam and Eve disobeyed God, they could no longer be in His presence without feeling embarrassed and fearful. But although God hates evil, He loves the sinner because God is love. For this reason, he is constantly looking for ways to demonstrate his love to His creation. He offers his forgiveness with limits to everyone who wants it. (John 3:16). Even the worst delinquents are objects of his holy love. He wants to save people and take them away from sin, because sin leads to death and eternal suffering, and God doesn't want that for His creations. On the contrary, God wants his children to share in his holiness (Isaiah 5:16; 6:1-7; 40:18-31).

## 5. God is triune.

The Bible reveals to us one God in three distinct persons: God the Father, Jesus Christ His Son, and the Holy Spirit. Although they are three different people, they are all the same one God.

It is not easy for us to understand this holy relationship between Father, Son, and Spirit. This is one of the mysteries where the Word keeps silent, and can only be accepted by faith. Every person can know the three persons of the God-head, experiencing the love, forgiveness and acceptance of the Father; to be saved by the grace of His Son, Jesus Christ and follow His perfect example in order to have eternal life; and have companionship with the Holy Spirit, who helps us live each day in the will of God (Matthew 3:16-17; 28:19-20; John 14:6-27; 1 Corinthians 8:6; 2 Corinthians 13:14; Galatians 4:4-6; Ephesians 2:13-18).

# II. JESUS CHRIST

**We believe** in Jesus Christ, the Second Person of the Triune Godhead; that He was eternally one with the Father; that He became incarnate by the Holy Spirit and was born of the Virgin Mary, so that two whole and perfect natures, *that is to say the Godhead and manhood, are thus united in one Person very God and very man, the God-man. We believe that Jesus Christ died for our sins, and that He truly arose from the dead and took again His body, together with all things appertaining to the perfection of man's nature, wherewith He ascended into heaven and is there engaged in intercession for us.*

**1. Faith in Jesus Christ is the distinctive belief of Christianity.** But not every group that calls itself Christian accepts the Christ that is revealed in the Bible. For example; the Jehovah Witnesses do not believe in the divinity of Christ; the Mormons deny that Jesus Christ was conceived by the Holy Spirit; the Roman Catholics, although they believe in the divinity of Christ, raise Mary to a place of intercessor that the Bible has not given to her, deflecting the believer's worship from the only mediator between God and man – Jesus Christ (Acts 4:10-12; 1 Tim. 2:5-6).

Some people believe that it is not important to God what kind of Christ or God one believes in, but only that the person is good and does good things. But this is not the truth, because God has taken the effort to reveal himself to mankind through His Word and His Living Word – Jesus Christ. The concept that the believer has of God and Christ is reflected in the way he feels, thinks, and acts towards God with his peers and with his surroundings. This article responds to the question: "According to the Bible, who is Jesus Christ and why did He come?"

**2. Jesus Christ has been one with the Father from all eternity.** The apostle John started his biography of Jesus affirming: "In the beginning was the Word, and the Word was with God, and the Word was God" (John 1:1). He continues writing in his gospel that this same Word, the only Son of God, who was from eternity with the Father[2], came to be born in order to become the only means by which mankind can receive eternal salvation (John 3:16).

In the New Testament, it is affirmed repeatedly that Christ is God, and frequently the authors make references to passages in the Old Testament where God is called "Lord" or in Hebrew "Yahweh".[3] But because of the second commandment (Exodus 20:7), the Jews were afraid to say this very sacred name, so they started to call Him "Lord" or in Greek "Kurios." When the first Christians (who had the Old Testament in Greek) called Christ "Lord," they were clearly referring to the same God. (Acts 2:21; Philippians 2:9)

Equally, the prophets of the Old Testament used "Lord" to refer to the coming Messiah, the Lamb of God who would be sent as the perfect sacrifice for the sins of all mankind. For example, Isaiah warned, "Prepare the way of the Lord..." (40:3).

There is no doubt in the biblical texts that Jesus Christ is God, that his life did no start at the moment of being conceived by the Holy Spirit in the Virgin Mary, but that He is God, divine member of the Trinity and that as such, is worthy to receive worship (Acts 7:59-60; Revelations 5:12-13) and forgive sins (Mark 2:5-10; Luke 5:20-24; Acts 5:31). As God, he possesses the unique characteristics of divinity that are mentioned in Article 1.

**3.  Jesus Christ the God Man.** Through the unrepeatable miracle in human history, one young lady named Mary, chosen by God, conceived in her womb a son in whom two natures was perfectly unified: divine and human (Mt. 1:18-25; Luke 1:26-38). His name would be Jesus or "Savior". The Son of God voluntarily chose to lay aside for a time the rights of being God, and humbled himself, taking the form of one of his creation (Phil. 2:5-8).

The gospels tell how these two natures coexisted in Jesus naturally. Neither of these natures annulled or did away with the other. As a man, he suffered hunger, thirst, fatigue, sleep, disappointment, pain, and experienced death. As God, he forgave sins, cast out demons, calmed the storm, and knew the intentions of people's hearts (Col. 1:12-22). As a man, he was tempted by Satan who tried to remove Him from the mission for which he had come (Matt. 4:1-11; Acts 4:15-16).

Denying the humanity of Christ is as dangerous as denying His deity, because it is in his humanity that he gave an example of how to live according to the will of God in the middle of a world contaminated by sin (Acts 2:22-36; 1 John 1:1-3, 4:2-3, 15).

**4.  Jesus Christ lived, died, and rose from the dead.** The name Jesus Christ expresses the unique nature of His mission.

Christ is the Greek word for Messiah, a word in Hebrew that pointed to the Lord, to God himself coming to this world to save mankind from sin and its consequences (Mt. 16:15-16). Jesus is the name of God incarnate and indicates the Savior.

So, the name of our Lord Jesus Christ reminds us that He is the Lord (God Himself), who came to be Jesus (the Savior) and thus free His people from the dominion of sin.

Jesus Christ fulfilled all aspects of this mission entrusted by God the Father for His first coming:

a. He revealed the truth about God to humanity "That the one who is the Word made himself flesh and lived among us, full of love and truth" (John 1:14).

b. He lived the truth that he taught, becoming the perfect model of a holy life for all generations of his disciples to imitate (Matt. 11:27; John 1:18, 14:9; Acts 1:1; 1 Peter 2:19-25).

c. He died to free all people from the dominion of sin (Mark 10:45). Since creation, divine justice had required for all who were contaminated with sin to be sentenced to eternal death and separation from the presence of God. This deserved condemnation for all of humanity could only be forgiven by the price that was demanded by divine justice: the shedding of innocent blood. This holy blood could not be provided by another human being, nor by an animal, since all of creation was subject to, and stained by, the evil of sin. God was the only one who could provide a holy Lamb, and the Lamb that was sent was Jesus Christ (2 Cor. 5:21).

d. He was resurrected, that is, His body died and then he was brought back to life to live forever (Matt. 28:6-7; Acts 10:39-40). Upon his resurrection, the Son of God returned to his place with the Father to continue his role as universal Lord of creation, taking back upon Himself the characteristics of deity that he had voluntarily laid aside when He came to earth (Rom. 8:32-34; Col. 3:1-3). His resurrection put an end to the power of death and the dominion of Satan over humanity (2 Cor. 5:14-15; Rev. 1:18). Upon ascending to heaven, Jesus Christ promised to return again to get all of His disciples of all generations and take them to live eternally with Him (John 14:1-3; 1 Tim. 6:14-16).

# III. THE HOLY SPIRIT

**We believe** *in the Holy Spirit, the Third Person of the Triune Godhead, that He is ever present and efficiently active in and with the Church of Christ, convincing the world of sin, regenerating those who repent and believe, sanctifying believers, and guiding into all truth as it is in Jesus.*

**1. The Holy Spirit is a Person.** This article of faith declares that according to the Bible, the Holy Spirit is a person of the divine trinity, and as such carries out a very important role for the Christian's salvation.

There are those who deny that the Holy Spirit is a person like the Father and the Son. The Jehovah's Witnesses, for example, affirm that the Holy Spirit is an influence or power exercised by God Himself. The Mormons teach that the Holy Spirit is an ethereal substance diffused through space. Some modern theologians say that it is the individual conscience. The Unitarian Church, for its part, affirms that it is a teacher that is inside of the believer substituting for the Bible, and that it can reveal new truths that Jesus did not teach.

**2. The Holy Spirit convicts of sin.** Without the help of the Holy Spirit, no person would feel sorrow for the sins he or she commits. Through the teaching, preaching, example and service to people, the church cooperates with the Holy Spirit in persuading and convincing sinners to repent of their sins and start to live as disciples of Christ (John 16:7-11; Rev. 22:17).

**3. The Holy Spirit renews those who repent.** Renew means to give new life, to make new. Those who repent of their sins, ask sincerely for God's forgiveness, and believe that the blood of Christ cleanses one from all sin are born into a new life. He or she no longer lives to satisfy their own selfish desires, but lives to serve God. It is the Holy Spirit who does this miracle in the heart of people, putting in them the desire to live far from the sin that before had enslaved them (John 3:1-6; Rom. 8:9).

**4. The Holy Spirit guides believers into truth (Rom. 8:14).** The Holy Spirit comes to live in new believers to guide the growth process in their new life in Christ (John 7:38-39; 1 Thess. 4:7-8; 1 John 3:24; 4:13). In order to carry out this purpose, He serves as: a counselor (John 14:26; 16:13); comforter (John 14:16); strengthens believers (Acts 9:31); imparts the love of God to believers (Eph. 3:14-21; Rom. 5:3-5); teaches them (1 Co. 12:3); among other things.

**5. The Holy Spirit sanctifies believers.** While growing in the knowledge of God, the Christian longs to live each day further away from sin and closer to Christ. It is the Holy Spirit who purifies the heart of the believer as a response to the unconditional surrender of his or her total being to the service of the Lord (John 14:16-17; Acts 16:8-9; 2 Tim. 2:13). This experience is explained in more detail in articles V and X.

**6. The Holy Spirit guides the Church in its mission to make Christlike disciples in all the nations** (Mt. 28:18-20). The Church must be sensitive to the Spirit, seeking direction for strategic planning for making disciples of Christ in their context, through prayer and the constant study of the Bible (Acts 9:31; 15:28).

# IV. THE HOLY SCRIPTURES ▬▬▬▬

**We believe** *in the plenary inspiration of the Holy Scriptures, by which we understand the 66 books of the Old and New Testaments, given by divine inspiration, inerrantly revealing the will of God concerning us in all things necessary to our salvation, so that whatever is not contained therein is not to be enjoined as an article of faith.*

1. The Church of the Nazarene believes that all of the Bible is the Word of God. Its authors were "inspired" by God, that is, they were guided by God Himself, in order to provide sufficient information to the human race so that they could live in obedience to the Creator. God has provided a reliable guide for each person who wants to live each day in holiness following the example of Jesus (Luke 14:44-47; 1 Cor. 15:3-4; 2 Tim. 3:15-17; 2 Peter 1:20-21). The biblical authors were not stripped of their personalities, neither were they indifferent to the historical situation that surrounded them. Because the authors communicated the message that they received from God to the people of their time, some people do not believe that the Biblical Message is relevant to this present time. However, although times change, sin continues being sin and the will of God for humans does not change, because God is the same yesterday, today, and forever. People can change, but the will of the Creator for people does not change.

Although the truth of God is unified, not all churches accept its authority as the sole standard of their faith. These churches provide authority for Christian faith and conduct from other sources, such as:

 a. Individual and personal experience.

 b. Experiences collected or gathered by generations of believers.

 c. Other sources of authority like opinions of church leaders or founders of a particular church.

2. Some examples of that are: the Roman Catholic Church considers that the words of the Popes are equal in authority with the Bible. Therefore they accept doctrines and practices that may not be based on biblical texts, such as the existence of purgatory or the worship of departed saints, among others. The same occurs with groups like Mormons or Jehovah Witnesses, who put the ideas or teachings of their founders in the same or higher level of authority than the Scriptures.

3. The Church of the Nazarene accepts as inspired by God the 66 books that are accepted by the other protestant churches. The Roman Catholic Church incorporates other books called "Apocrypha," meaning uninspired.

## V. SIN, ORIGINAL AND PERSONAL

**We believe** *that sin came into the world through the disobedience of our first parents, and death by sin. We believe that sin is of two kinds: original sin or depravity, and actual or personal sin.*

*a)* **We believe** *that original sin, or depravity, is that corruption of the nature of all the offspring of Adam by reason of which everyone is very far gone from original righteousness or the pure state of our first parents at the time of their creation, is averse to God, is without spiritual life, and inclined to evil, and that continually. We further believe that original sin continues to exist with the new life of the regenerate, until the heart is fully cleansed by the baptism with the Holy Spirit.*

*b)* **We believe** *that original sin differs from actual sin in that it constitutes an inherited propensity to actual sin for which no one is accountable until its divinely provided remedy is neglected or rejected.*

*c)* **We believe** *that actual or personal sin is a voluntary violation of a known law of God by a morally responsible person. It is therefore not to be confused with involuntary and inescapable shortcomings, infirmities, faults, mistakes, failures, or other deviations from a standard of perfect conduct that are the residual effects of the Fall. However, such innocent effects do not include attitudes or responses contrary to the spirit of Christ, which may properly be called sins of the spirit. We believe that personal sin is primarily and essentially a violation of the law of love;*

**1. Original sin.** Every human being shares a common inheritance that consists of a desire or inclination toward evil (evil is the opposite of the will of God). Every human is born tainted by the sin of Adam and Eve, the first parents (Gen. 2:16-17; Psalms 51:5). The Bible teaches that sin is like a lethal sickness, consuming human beings, causing them to not only die physically, but also to die spiritually (Rom. 5:12).

When sin entered the human race, the original purity that God had given to the man and woman when he made them in His image and likeness was broken. We can understand this better if we compare Adam and Eve with mirrors that reflect the divine perfection in your life. Sin was the stone that broke those mirrors, leaving only pieces or remnants of that "image of God" that he had given them. This image of God has not been completely lost. That is why people without Christ can do good things, like love, forgive, feel compassion, help those who suffer, do charity works, etc.

The individual conscience is another aspect of the image of God that at times functions as a brake to this tendency to do evil. This conscience, although it is tainted or contaminated with original sin, on occasions warns people and accuses them of their wrong doing. But human beings who want to continue doing evil can ignore or minimize this interior voice until they silence it completely.

Alongside these remaining vestiges of the original purity inherited from the Creator, there coexists the tendency to do evil that is inherited from our human parents (Mark 7:21-23). It is not true, as some claim, that human beings are essentially good and that sin is learned through socio-cultural environments (1 John 1:7-8). This is evident in observing the behavior of a small child: Who teaches the child to disobey?

Why do small children hide the truth from their parents when they know that they had done something wrong?

Although human beings are not responsible for this sinful nature, they are responsible for searching for a solution to be free from it. In His Word, God affirms that human beings cannot be free of this nature simply by trying. The only solution to this condition is provided by the Creator who, wanting to restore in us that original image of purity, imparts His holiness to us (1 Cor. 15:22).

The remedy for this problem that God has provided in Christ Jesus will be explained in more detail in articles VI and X.

**2. Personal sin.** Sin is everything that a person voluntarily thinks, says, or does that is contrary to the will of God. Sin is evil because it offends the holiness of God, raising a barrier between people and their creator. It destroys God's perfect plan for their lives now and for eternity.

When a person does something that is contrary to the desires of God, it is generally said that he did something "bad" because he did a wrong action, freely choosing to do the wrong or evil instead of doing what he knows is correct or good. (Compare Matt. 22:36-40 with 1 John 3:4). But for God, personal sin is not only bad actions, but also includes all those internal thoughts and feelings of the heart and mind that precede those sinful actions.

If a vender charges someone for a kilo of bread knowing that the scale is bad and that the weight is really only 850 grams, he is deceiving and robbing his customer. Those are actions that result from his internal hidden motives. These motives come to light if the behavior is examined by some simple questions: Why is he deceiving and robbing? Why does he continue doing that? What personal benefit can be found? Perhaps the answer is greed or excessive ambition. Greed and excessive ambition are also sin in God's eyes.

That's why the Word of God defines personal sin as follows:
a. Evil desires, like wanting what is not ours, lust for power and/or prestige, etc.
b. Evil feelings, like hate, envy, bitterness, greed, etc.
c. Bad attitudes, like mistreating others, discriminating against people because of their race, gender, age, religion, or other reason, etc.
d. Bad thoughts, like thinking bad of a person without

reason, lustful thoughts, jealousy, etc.

e. Bad words, like lies, insults, profanity, making fun of God and His Word, etc.

f. Doing wrong.

Every person who is living or has lived on this planet has committed some of these sins (Rom. 3:10). Every human being would be forever lost if not for the remedy provided by God: Jesus Christ, who lived a sinless life and took the place on the cross that belonged to each of the sinners of this world (Romans 3:23.). This is discussed more in Articles VI and IX.

# VI. ATONEMENT

*We believe that Jesus Christ, by His sufferings, by the shedding of His own blood, and by His death on the Cross, made a full atonement for all human sin, and that this Atonement is the only ground of salvation, and that it is sufficient for every individual of Adam's race. The Atonement is graciously efficacious for the salvation of those incapable of moral responsibility and for the children in innocency but is efficacious for the salvation of those who reach the age of responsibility only when they repent and believe.*

**1. Salvation is available for everyone.** The salvation offered by God through His Son Jesus Christ is for everyone who believes in Jesus Christ and follows Him (John 3:16). Salvation is a gift that God offers by his grace, that is, by his great love. This love cannot be bought, won, or deserved. God's grace is a gift He offers to every human being.

**2. Atonement.** The word "atonement" expresses the merciful action of God when he forgives the repentant sinner, and erases from his life all the sins that he has committed by shifting to Christ the blame and punishment those sins deserved. (Isaiah 53:5, 6, 11; Mark 10:45; Rom. 6:21-23; Gal. 1:3-4; 3:13-14; 1 Tim. 2:3-6; Heb. 2:9; 1 John 2:1-2). In some translations of the Bible, the word "atonement" is replaced by "propitiation" which has the same meaning (Rom. 3:21-26). In that moment, the person becomes free of the penalty of their sins and recovers their relationship of friendship with the Holy Creator. (1 Cor. 6:20; 2 Cor. 5:14-21; Col. 1:19-23).

For the Jews of the Old and New Testaments, this idea of transferring personal sin to an innocent being was well understood. In the Hebrew sacrificial system of worship, every repentant person brought an unblemished lamb to the priest to be sacrificed in their place. But the blood of those animals could not erase the offense of the sin of humans. Those sacrifices could only anticipate that God, in His appointed time, would send the perfect lamb, Jesus Christ, to give himself as a sacrifice for the sin of all humanity. (John 1:29; John 3:17; Rom. 5:6-21; 1 Pet. 1:18-21).

**3. The Innocent.** Who did God free from the guilt of sin? The Bible declares that God will not acquit the guilty (Nahum 1:3). Also, the opposite is true: God does not hold the innocent guilty. Among the innocent (or people who are not guilty for the bad things that they have done) are children (Matt. 18:3; 19:14); people who insane or who have illnesses that keep them from distinguishing the good from the bad.

# VII. PREVENIENT GRACE

**We believe** *that the grace of God through Jesus Christ is freely bestowed upon all people, enabling all who will to turn from sin to righteousness, believe on Jesus Christ for pardon and cleansing from sin, and follow good works pleasing and acceptable in His sight. We also believe that the human race's creation in Godlikeness included the ability to choose between right and wrong, and that thus human beings were made morally responsible; that through the fall of Adam they became depraved so that they cannot now turn and prepare themselves by their own natural strength and works to faith and calling upon God.*

**1. Divine grace is the free favor of God toward humans.** It is by God's grace, and not by personal effort, that we can obtain divine forgiveness for sinful actions and be cleansed from original sin. (Eph. 2:2-9; Tit. 2:11 -14; 3:4-7)

**2. God's grace works in people before they repent.** Jesus Christ taught his disciples that the influence of the Holy Spirit starts in the lives of people before they are saved. The Spirit helps the sinner, drawing him to Christ, convincing him of sin and instilling faith so that he can put all his trust in the Lord's sacrifice on his behalf (John 16:8-9). It is the Spirit that regenerates the new disciple of Christ, imparting to him the life of Christ and accompanying him in all of his life, teaching him to live according to God's will. It is the Holy Spirit who administers the divine grace. This point will be explained in article VIII.

**3. Once one has been forgiven, how must they live to keep from losing their salvation?** God's will for all of his children is that they live holy lives (1 Pet. 3:15). A Christian who remains living in sin must repent and turn from those sins or he will lose his salvation and eternal life (Phil. 2:12; 1 Cor. 9:27). The promise of eternal life is for everyone who perseveres as disciples of Christ until the end of their lives (Rev. 2:10).

**4. To apostatize means to abandon the faith** and return to the sinful life, separating yourself from Christ and the family of God (the church).

# VIII. REPENTANCE

**We believe** *the Spirit of God gives to all who will repent the gracious help of penitence of heart and hope of mercy, that they may believe unto pardon and spiritual life. Repentance, which is a sincere and thorough change of the mind in regard to sin, involving a sense of personal guilt and a voluntary turning away from sin, is demanded of all who have by act or purpose become sinners against God.*

**We believe** *that all persons may fall from grace and apostatize and, unless they repent of their sins, be hopelessly and eternally lost. We believe that regenerate persons need not return to sin but may live in unbroken fellowship with God through the power of the indwelling Holy Spirit who bears witness with our spirits that we are children of God.*

**1. What is repentance?** Repentance is feeling pain for the sins that you have committed, asking forgiveness from God for having offended Him, changing your attitude by making a sincere decision to abandon the sinful life and to start living a new life with God (Luke 13:3; Acts 3:19; 1 John 1:9).

**2. What must a person do who has already been forgiven but sins again?** When a disciple of Christ sins, or choses voluntarily to do that which is evil in the eyes of God, they must repent and ask forgiveness for that sin, and if there were others affected by their sin, they must also ask forgiveness from them as well.

# IX. JUSTIFICATION, REGENERATION, AND ADOPTION

**We believe** *that justification is the gracious and judicial act of God by which He grants full pardon of all guilt and complete release from the penalty of sins committed, and acceptance as righteous, to all who believe on Jesus Christ and receive Him as Lord and Savior.*

**We believe** *that regeneration, or the new birth, is that gracious work of God whereby the moral nature of the repentant believer is spiritually quickened and given a distinctively spiritual life, capable of faith, love, and obedience.*

**We believe** *that adoption is that gracious act of God by which the justified and regenerated believer is constituted a child of God.*

**We believe** *that justification, regeneration, and adoption are simultaneous in the experience of seekers after God and are received by faith, preceded by repentance; and that to this work and state of grace the Holy Spirit bears witness.*

**1.  This article is about what God does to restore the repentant sinner.** This first experience of reconciliation with God is also called the first work of grace, in order to distinguish it from entire sanctification, which is explained in Article X.

**2.  Justification.** Justification is the complete forgiveness of God for the sins that a person has committed up to the moment of repentance. God gives us the opportunity to start again, free of the penalty of our own sins. Those sins are erased and God forgets them (Psalm 32:1; Micah 7:19; Luke 18:13-14; Romans 5:1; Acts 10:17). Then, the repentant sinner is declared righteous, freeing him from the punishment that his disobedience deserves (Acts 13:38-39; Gal. 2:16).

**3.  Regeneration.** Every human being has been endowed with a spirit that survives physical death. The Bible affirms that those who live in sin are spiritually dead because they are separated from God. So, as the Apostle Paul said, one can be alive to his family and friends, but is dead to God. One's human spirit is destined to eternal death and will not be regenerated or brought to life by God. In order for the spirit to be born again, it must first "die," which means that one must leave sin behind and start to live life with Christ. (Rom. 6:11- 13; Eph. 2:1-10).

When a person is regenerated, his life changes completely. It's not just an exterior change, like acquiring new habits of conduct or leaving behind some bad things that you used to do. It is a complete change brought about in the person's heart that little by little transforms his entire being. This experience is also called "conversion," because the regenerated person's life is centered in Christ. Before, he lived for himself, but now, he lives for God and serves Him with his life (2 Cor. 5:14-21).

When a person has been regenerated, the transformation is evident to everyone. Some people want to be justified but don't want to be regenerated because they don't want to abandon their past habits that prevent them from living as Christ's disciples.

On occasion in Christian churches, one can find those who instead of being converted are "convinced." It is easy to recognize them because they believe in Christ, and they like to attend church, but like the rich young ruler, they are not willing to allow Christ to transform their whole being and life (Matt. 19:16-30). Others search for divine forgiveness only to free themselves from the guilt that torments them, or to obtain a favor from God (work, health, etc...), but they don't permit the Lord to transform their entire being. God regenerates everyone who wishes the new life that He offers in Christ.

**4. Adoption.** Adoption is the act by which God adopts the regenerate person, making them his son or daughter and a member of His family – the Church (John 1:11-13; Rom. 8:15-17; Gal. 4:3-7; I John 3:4-10). The regenerate person can call God Father and enjoy fellowship with Holy God. No sinner can have this close relationship with God, nor call Him Father. The Holy Spirit comes to live in the heart of the regenerate person and communicates with his/her human spirit giving them the assurance that they are a child of God (Rom. 8:16-17; Acts 10:19-22).

# X. CHRISTIAN HOLINESS AND ENTIRE SANCTIFICATION

**We believe** *that sanctification is the work of God which transforms believers into the likeness of Christ. It is wrought by God's grace through the Holy Spirit in initial sanctification, or regeneration (simultaneous with justification), entire sanctification, and the continued perfecting work of the Holy Spirit culminating in glorification. In glorification we are fully conformed to the image of the Son.*

**We believe** *that entire sanctification is that act of God, subsequent to regeneration, by which believers are made free from original sin, or depravity, and brought into a state of entire devotement to God, and the holy obedience of love made perfect.*

*It is wrought by the baptism with or infilling of the Holy Spirit, and comprehends in one experience the cleansing of the heart from sin and the abiding, indwelling presence of the Holy Spirit, empowering the believer for life and service. Entire sanctification is provided by the blood of Jesus, is wrought instantaneously by grace through faith, preceded by entire consecration; and to this work and state of grace the Holy Spirit bears witness.*

*This experience is also known by various terms representing its different phases, such as "Christian perfection," "perfect love," "heart unity," "the baptism with or infilling of the Holy Spirit," "the fullness of the blessing," and "Christian holiness."*

**We believe** *that there is a marked distinction between a pure heart and a mature character. The former is obtained in an instant, the result of entire sanctification; the latter is the result of growth in grace.*

**We believe** *that the grace of entire sanctification includes the divine impulse to grow in grace as a Christlike disciple. However, this impulse must be consciously nurtured, and careful attention given to the requisites and processes of spiritual development and improvement in Christlikeness of character and personality. Without such purposeful* *endeavor, one's witness may be impaired and the grace itself frustrated and ultimately lost.*

*Participating in the means of grace, especially the fellowship, disciplines, and sacraments of the Church, believers grow in grace and in wholehearted love to God and neighbor.*

**1. The will of God is that the Christian lives in purity in this life.** The Church of the Nazarene believes that without entire sanctification, it is impossible to live a holy life and reach the goal of eternal life. (John 17:9,17, 20). Not all churches believe in the baptism of the Holy Spirit in the same way. Some for example understand that entire sanctification of the Christian only occurs after physical death.

Nazarenes believe that there is a moment in which the disciple of Christ understands the need to be freed from this sinful condition that battles inside against their desire to be totally obedient to their Lord.

This sinful condition prompts them to seek their own selfish desires instead of seeking first the will of God. The Christian that lives in this battle feels guilty of these evil inclinations which they cannot stop. (Psalm 51:7; Acts 15:8-9; Eph. 5:25-27; 1 John 1:7).

At times, this state of dissatisfaction with themselves leads them to doubt their experience of salvation. Satan takes advantage of this doubt by tempting them and trying to separate them from Christ.

God has provided a solution for this problem for everyone who voluntarily hands over complete control of their life to Jesus Christ (consecration), and by faith asks that God completely purifies their heart, fills them with His Holy Spirit, and takes complete control of their life (Rom. 12:1-2; 1 Thes. 5:23-24).

**2. Changes produced by the Holy Spirit.** When the Holy Spirit in-fills the disciple of Christ, God pours His holy love into them. This love increasingly motivates them to live a life of service to God and to their neighbors (Matt. 3:11-12; 2 Thes. 2:13-14). This Christian can see some big changes in their life, such as:

    a.  More strength to overcome temptations (Phil. 4:13; 2 Tim. 1:7);

b. A fervent desire to have opportunities to talk to others about Christ (John 15:26-27; Acts 1:8);

c. Courage to fulfill the ministry to which God has called them (Acts 4:31; 6:8; 7:55-60);

d. The desire to seek more and more of Christ - to know him, obey him, and search for his will in everything, even the smallest thing (Rom. 8:26; Col. 1:10-12).

**3. Should we expect an external sign to be sure that we have received entire sanctification?** The Church of the Nazarene does not find any biblical basis to believe that one must wait for an external sign (like speaking in other languages or with incomprehensible sounds) to show that they have been filled with the Holy Spirit.

On the Day of Pentecost, when the disciples spoke in strange languages, that is, languages and dialects that they had not previously learned, God was enabling them to communicate the gospel in words understood by everyone who heard them. This miracle enabled the spread of the gospel to many different nations and people (Acts 2:6-11). This miracle was repeated in other occasions in which the language was a barrier in making disciples of Christ (Acts 10:19).

In 1 Cor. 12 and 13, Paul mentions that there were Christians in the city of Corinth who spoke different languages, and others who served God as translators or interpreters, so that the gospel could be preached and taught. This was considered to be a spiritual gift (the Greek word that Paul used was "charisma"). But in chapter 14, Paul mentions that in this church, there were also some in the congregation who were speaking a language that nobody could understand. However, this did not qualify as a spiritual gift since no one could understand what was said and there wasn't anyone who could interpret it. Therefore, it did not serve to edify or build up the church (1 Cor. 14:12-19). Paul did not encourage them to continue practicing this type of language, but rather to dedicate themselves to preaching or other spiritual gifts, instead of being preoccupied with something that did not help the church grow (1 Cor. 14:1-11).

The only church of the New Testament that practiced this strange language was the one in Corinth, a church that Paul criticized for being "carnal" (1 Cor. 3:1-4). A carnal believer is one who puts their own selfish interests before God's will. Those believers didn't have the Spirit of Christ in them, and they didn't have love, although they did make a lot of noise (1 Cor. 13). Also, they were called "children" who insisted on speaking incomprehensible languages rather than attracting others to Christ by speaking languages that people could understand. Because of that, people began to think that Christians were crazy (14:20-23). Paul encouraged them instead to dedicate themselves to preaching and all that would edify the church (14:24-26).

There also isn't any biblical evidence to support the idea that Christians need a special language in order to pray, as some churches practice (1 Cor. 14:13-16). The Bible doesn't mention that Jesus practiced this. When the disciples asked Jesus to teach them to pray, he didn't mention this special type of language (Luke 11:1-4). Instead, Jesus encouraged his followers to pray, speaking with God as a child speaks with his Father (Luke 11:5-13).

**4. We must not confuse purity with Christian maturity,** although one proceeds from the other. Those who have received the fullness of the Holy Spirit have been cleansed by God from the impurity of sin for a purpose. God wants to reproduce in them the holy life of Jesus. Purification is instantaneous, it occurs in a moment, but the growth toward maturity is progressive. So, the Christian never stops being perfected. One should be able to see positives changes in different aspects of your life from before you were filled to after you were filled with the Holy Spirit. The entirely sanctified Christian must never stop growing, maturing, and reflecting Jesus Christ more and more in his being (Phil. 3:12-15; 2 Cor. 3:17-18).

# XI. THE CHURCH

**We believe** in the Church, the community that confesses Jesus Christ as Lord, the covenant people of God made new in Christ, the Body of Christ called together by the Holy Spirit through the Word.

God calls the Church to express its life in the unity and fellowship of the Spirit; in worship through the preaching of *the Word, observance of the sacraments, and ministry in His name; by obedience to Christ, holy living, and mutual accountability.*

*The mission of the Church in the world is to share in the redemptive and reconciling ministry of Christ in the power of the Spirit. The Church fulfills its mission by making disciples through evangelism, education, showing compassion, working for justice, and bearing witness to the kingdom of God.*

*The Church is a historical reality that organizes itself in culturally conditioned forms, exists both as local congregations and as a universal body, and also sets apart persons called of God for specific ministries. God calls the Church to live under His rule in anticipation of the consummation at the coming of our Lord Jesus Christ.*

**1. Who is the Church?** The Church of Christ is one, and is composed of all the disciples of all ages (Matt. 18:20; Acts 2:47; 1 Cor. 12:13; Eph. 4:4-6; Rev. 7:9-10). Through the ages, the Christian Church has been divided by many reasons: by doctrinal differences, by differences in worship styles, by geographical or cultural distances, among others. Therefore, it is necessary to differentiate between the church that is universal and outside of denominations, from the local church or denominations, which are groups of disciples of Christ in a community or geographical region. Today, there are many Christian churches which coexist with different names, and this has caused confusion among some people. Certain churches have a sound doctrine based on the Bible, but others interpret the Word of God lightly and teach doctrines of man mixed with the revealed truth. One can tell if a church is centered in the Word when you see how their leaders and members live (Acts 20:28).

**2. A healthy church.** The Church of the Nazarene is a church that in concerned that its leaders, pastors, and members around the world receive healthy teaching, centered in Christ, that helps them live a holy life following in the footsteps of Jesus (Eph. 5:25-26).

**3. A church that serves.** It is expected that every member of the Churches of the Nazarene will actively participate in the mission of making disciples of Christ, by using their material, intellectual, and spiritual resources for God's service (Acts 8:4).

# XII. BAPTISM

**We believe** *that Christian baptism, commanded by our Lord, is a sacrament signifying acceptance of the benefits of the atonement and incorporation into the Body of Christ. Baptism is a means of grace proclaiming faith in Jesus Christ as Savior. It is to be administered to believers indicating their full purpose of obedience in holiness and righteousness. As participants in the new covenant, young children and the morally innocent may be baptized upon request of parents or guardians. The church shall give assurance of Christian training. Baptism may be administered by sprinkling, pouring, or immersion.*

**1. It is the Lord's command.** The Lord Jesus commanded his disciples to baptize all new believers (Mark 16:16).

**2. The time of baptism.** In the New Testament times, believers were often baptized almost immediately after their conversion (Acts 22:16). Today, most churches wait for a reasonable time to give the new disciple an opportunity to understand the significance of this sacrament.

**3. It is the testimony of God's grace.** Baptism is a testimony of at least three things that have occurred previously:

   a. The person being baptized has repented of their sins and has shown their desire to live as a disciple of Christ.

   b. God, by His grace, has forgiven them and has resurrected them to a new life.

   c. God has joined His new child to His family (the church), which accepts the responsibility delegated by Christ to disciple them, to live as examples for them, and integrate them into the ministry of the local church.

**4. There are three forms of baptism that the Church of the Nazarene practices:**

   a. Immersion is completely submerging the person in water (Rom. 6:3-5).

   b. Sprinkling is spraying or splashing water over the head of the new Christian (Acts 16:33).

   c. Affusion consists of pouring a little water on the head of the person (Acts 1:5; 2:17; 33; 10:45).

# XIII. THE LORD'S SUPPER

**We believe** *that the Communion Supper instituted by our Lord and Savior Jesus Christ is a sacrament, proclaiming His life, sufferings, sacrificial death, resurrection, and the hope of His coming again. The Lord's Supper is a means of grace in which Christ is present by the Spirit. All are invited to participate by faith in Christ and be renewed in life, salvation, and in unity as the Church. All are to come in reverent appreciation of its significance, and by it show forth the Lord's death until He comes. Those who have faith in Christ and love for the saints are invited by Christ to participate as often as possible.*

**1. The symbolism of the bread and the grape juice.** The last night before the crucifixion, Jesus Christ and his disciples ate together. It was the time of the Jewish festival of the Passover, when the people remembered what occurred the night before God liberated the slaves from Egypt.

On this occasion, as Jesus divided the bread and distributed the grape juice to his disciples, he reminded them that he was going to be sacrificed for the sins of all of humanity. He used those symbols so that they could understand that his body was going to be tortured and his blood would be poured out so that they could be saved, forever freed from the slavery of sin (Luke 22:7-23).

**2. It was commanded by the Lord.** On that occasion, Jesus asked them to celebrate this ritual in order to never forget that which He was about to do for them and for everyone who would believe in Him. This would be a symbol of the union of the Church with her Lord forever. Jesus has promised to celebrate this dinner with all of His disciples from all ages and all nations at His second coming (Matt. 22:19-20).

**3. Christ is the Lord of His Church.** These symbols also remind us that Christ is the Lord of the Church, and that He gave Himself up for it, in order to cleanse it from sin with his blood and prepare her in holiness to live eternally with Holy God (1 Cor. 11:23-26).

# XIV. DIVINE HEALING

**We believe** *in the biblical doctrine of divine healing and urge our people to offer the prayer of faith for the healing of the sick. We also believe God heals through the means of medical science.*

**1. Disease was not a creation of God.** The Church of the Nazarene believes that God is the source of physical health, and that it is not His will that people suffer because of sicknesses. Diseases were not introduced into the world by God, but came as a consequence of the sin of humankind. Disease will not touch God's children in the eternal life that He has promised them (Rev. 22:2).

**2. Jesus and the sick.** Christians must have the same compassion for the sick that Jesus had, and do everything in their power to alleviate suffering. Jesus saw sick people as an opportunity to show the love of God to them (Matt. 4:23). Jesus' concern for the sick opened their ears to hear the good news of salvation (Matt. 4:23).

**3. Prayer for the sick must be done with faith and compassion.** But first, we must be prepared to accept the will of God, regardless of what it may be. If God does a miracle, the person must be encouraged to not keep it a secret, but share it with everyone so that they will open their hearts to the Lord (James 5:13-15).

**4. God can also heal through treatments of medical science.** Therefore, we must not delay in consulting with these professionals, even though we always ask God to guide them in what they do. Doctors are in the best position to give evidence of a miracle, and God also wants them to give their hearts to Jesus. The author of the Gospel of Luke and the book of Acts was the personal doctor and disciple of the apostle Paul.

**5. When God doesn't heal his children.** At times, God doesn't heal his children but allows them to suffer from sickness and physical disability. Even though at times He does not reveal his reason for why He permits this, they must trust that there is a holy purpose for all that God does in their lives. In these cases, the believer has the special help that God has promised to endure the difficulties. (Rom. 8:28; II Cor. 12:7-10).

# XV. SECOND COMING OF CHRIST ▨▨▨

**We believe** *that the Lord Jesus Christ will come again; that we who are alive at His coming shall not precede them that are asleep in Christ Jesus; but that, if we are abiding in Him, we shall be caught up with the risen saints to meet the Lord in the air, so that we shall ever be with the Lord.*

**1. The second coming.** Jesus Christ will return again in all His power and glory to seek out those who are his own (His Church), and punish forever all those who have refused to live in obedience to the holy will of the Creator (Acts 1:11).

**2. Joy for some and suffering for others.** It will be a time of infinite joy for all the Christians who have died (they will be resurrected), and for those who are living. But for all those who have rejected the Lord, it will be a time of great despair (1 Thess. 4:13-18).

# XVI. RESURRECTION, ▨▨▨ JUDGMENT, AND DESTINY

**We believe** *in the resurrection of the dead, that the bodies both of the just and of the unjust shall be raised to life and united with their spirits—"they that have done good, unto the resurrection of life; and they that have done evil, unto the resurrection of damnation."*

**We believe** *in future judgment in which every person shall appear before God to be judged according to his or her deeds in this life.*

**We believe** *that glorious and everlasting life is assured to all who savingly believe in, and obediently follow, Jesus Christ our Lord; and that the finally impenitent shall suffer eternally in hell.*

**1. Every human being will one day stand before God to be judged.** This judgment will occur only one time in history and will be after the second coming of Christ. It will be a judgment of punishment but also of reward (Acts 17:30-31; 2 Cor. 5:10, Heb. 9:27-28).

**2. Will there be some opportunity after death to repent?**
The Bible does not teach that there will be an opportunity after death to be reconciled with the Creator. This life is all the time that a person has to respond to the call of God for repentance and holy living (John 5:20-29).

**3. The urgency of evangelism.** Since it is not possible to receive God's forgiveness after death, every disciple of Christ is responsible before God to evangelize and disciple their generation, since each person that dies without Christ is forever lost and their eternal destiny is suffering forever in hell.

# References

1. When "God" is written with a capital "G," it refers to the one true God. When it is written with a small "g," it refers to false gods.

2. In other words, John affirmed that Christ had participated as part of the Trinity in the creation of the world. See Genesis 1 and Hebrews 11:3 that the universe came into existence through the Word of God. The Holy Spirit was also present at creation (Gen. 1:2).

3. In some translations, "Jehova" is mistakenly translated as "Yahweh," but "Jehova" does not have a Hebrew origin but only started to be used early in the 16th century.

# Bibliography

Anderson, Ken, Where to Find it in the Bible

Fisher, C. William, Why are You an Evangelical?

Manual Church of the Nazarene 2017-2021

Knight, John A., What the Bible Says about the Gift of Tongues

Purkiser, W. T, Adventures in Biblical Doctrine

Taylor, R., Grider, J.K., Taylor, W., Beacon Theological Dictionary

# LOVING LIKE JESUS DID

C. Helmer Juárez

## INTRODUCTION

Loving our neighbor is a basic concept of the Christian life.

When we begin our relationship with God, many issues on which we may have based our previous life will change gradually. As a result, our life-style will also begin to be transformed, bringing an important change of attitude towards our fellow men, the people with whom we relate, those among whom we live.

One of the important changes that will come with the new life in Christ can be seen in the way we love others. In some ways it seems easier to love God than to love others. It is easy to love God, for although we do not see Him, we know what He has done for us. On the contrary, it is not easy to love our neighbors who are often annoying, impertinent, never satisfied, and whom we also see almost every day reminding us of their imperfections.

Nevertheless, one of the most important keys to success in the Christian life is to "love our neighbor"; the Bible warns us that we cannot say that we love God if we do not love our neighbor (1 John 4:8.21).

In this short volume, we want to summarize some concepts that will help us understand why God asks us to love our neighbor, and how this love becomes a visible proof of the change God is making in our lives.

We will try to walk through some biblical concepts as well as look at Jesus' example to help us understand what this kind of love for our neighbors that God expects of us looks like.

Within the Church of the Nazarene we recognize that God commands us to love our fellow men, and we want learn to love like Jesus did, which is the hallmark of the lifestyle of the Global Nazarene church.

# THE COMMANDMENT OF LOVE ▰▰▰▰

If we truly want to be "Christians", not only in name but in truth, then we must understand and practice the "command-ment of love".

In Matthew 22:37-39 we find these words of Jesus, "'Love the Lord your God with all your heart and with all your soul and with all your mind.' This is the first and greatest commandment. And the second is like it, 'Love your neighbor as yourself.'" From the beginning, this "love" has been the essence of the Christian life and can be defined as, human love responding in obedience to the redemptive love[1] of God.

As human beings, we almost always see the commandment of love in two parts, first loving God, and then secondly loving our neighbor. We are inclined to want to love God but we forget our neighbor.

God invites us to love others with a kind of unselfish love that has four distinguishing characteristics:

**1. To love God with all our heart:** This implies loving with devotion, that is, keeping God always present in our thoughts and giving Him the supreme place in our lives. It is a love characterized by faithfulness; a love to which we commit ourselves daily, continuously. This also implies loving Him with our feelings and passion. To love with the whole heart implies to involve all our emotions. When we have God in our hearts, it is not difficult to love Him because our heart naturally responds to His love.

**2. Love God with your entire mind:** This refers to loving Him with all our intellectual ability. Our ability to reason and to understand can help us to know God and understand His way of seeing things. The more we know about Him, the more we love Him, and the more we love Him, the more we want to know Him. We need to fill our minds with the Word of God which will help us to understand better the needs of those around us, enabling us to love and serve them better. Our mind, committed to God, will have much wisdom and knowledge to share.

**3. We must also love God with all strength:** This involves showing love in everything we do. The Christian lifestyle should be evident in all areas of our lives: in business, at work, in dealing with our spouses and children, among others.

When we love God in this way, we will also love our neighbor as a result of the love of God dwelling in our lives.

Loving our neighbor is not option for the Christian, but a commandment that we should strive to obey. We must allow God to change our lives, replacing selfishness with freedom to love all people in the same way that we love ourselves.

## WHO IS OUR NEIGHBOR?

¿Should I help everyone, or only those who like me? Whom should I help? Just the ones I have around? The one who lives next to my house? Or just my relatives or friends? Who is my neighbor? These are the questions we often ask ourselves when it comes to helping others. The questions do not have easy answers. It is very difficult to decide who our neighbors are.

In Jesus' time, there were people who were also uneasy about this question. In Luke chapter 10, we find a story that Jesus used to answer this question. He told about a Jewish man who was traveling when he was attacked by thieves who stole everything he was carrying, beat him, wounded him and left him half dead. Two Jewish religious leaders passed by and did not help him. Then a stranger, a Samaritan, passed by (Samaritan were not supposed to be friends of the Jews). But this stranger got off his horse, took care of the injured man, and took him to an inn (hotel for travelers). There he asked the owner to take care of the man, and he paid the whole bill, even giving instructions that they should spare no expense to attend to the wounded man. If it was necessary, he would return and pay for whatever extra cost had been incurred.

Jesus asked at the end of the story: Who was the neighbor of the wounded man? Those who heard did not want to acknowledge that it was the Samaritan, but this was evident since it was he who had mercy on the wounded traveler. Jesus told them to follow the example of this good man.

So who is my neighbor? According to this account, my neighbor is every person who crosses my path and has a need of any kind. In other words, every person we have opportunity to help to change their current situation of suffering and hopelessness.

The command of Jesus is quite clear. We must serve others

in all we can, not only those who are close to us, or who we like, or who could later pay us for help, but all men, women and children to whom we have opportunity to help.

## WHY SHOULD WE LOVE ▬▬▬ OUR NEIGHBOR?

Throughout the Bible, God demands all his children to have compassion for their fellow people, just as He had compassion on us.

Essentially, our God is a God who loves all human beings. In John 3:16, we find a statement from Jesus that speaks of God's love for us: "For God so loved the world that he gave his one and only Son, that whoever believes in him shall not perish but have eternal life."

From the Old Testament times, God has endeavored to show us His love and to motivate us to practice this same kind of selfless love for one another. One of the greatest stories of God's love is how He met all the needs of his people during the 40-year journey from Egypt to the land of Israel. Here are some examples:

1. God made their clothes last: Deuteronomy 8:4 says, "Your clothes did not wear out and your feet did not swell during these forty years."

2. God fed them with bread and meat: When the people became hungry, he supplied them with manna[2] and also with quail meat[3].

But just as God took care of them, he also charged them to take care of others. This can be found in Deuteronomy 24:17-22 where God points out some of the neighbors who they should take care of:

1. Foreigners and orphans: "Do not deprive the foreigner or the fatherless of justice," meaning that they should not take advantage of them or treat them badly.

2. Widows: "or take the cloak of the widow as a pledge," that is, they should not take advantage of the widow's need by taking away her belongings.

3. They should share their possessions with the needy: "When you are harvesting in your field and you

overlook a sheaf, do not go back to get it. Leave it for the foreigner, the fatherless and the widow." This commandment had a promise of blessing from God, "so that the Lord your God may bless you in all the work of your hands."

4. Sharing with the destitute: Deuteronomy 15:7 says, "If anyone is poor among your fellow Israelites in any of the towns of the land the Lord your God is giving you, do not be hardhearted or tightfisted toward them."

These are just a few examples of the Old Testament commandments, there are many more. In the New Testament we find new teachings on love of neighbor.

Jesus our Savior, who is our supreme example of love and compassion, left us several valuable lessons and examples.

During his ministry, "Jesus went throughout Galilee, teaching in their synagogues, proclaiming the good news of the kingdom, and healing every disease and sickness among the people" (Matthew 4:23). Jesus did not just stay in the temple, but went through all the towns and cities, and as He preached and taught, he took care of the physical needs of people such as sickness and hunger, among others.

Matthew 9:36 says that Jesus "had compassion on them, because they were harassed and helpless, like sheep without a shepherd." Matthew 14:14 says that when Jesus "saw a large crowd, he had compassion on them and healed their sick."

Matthew 15:32 tells us that "Jesus called his disciples to him and said, "I have compassion for these people; they have already been with me three days and have nothing to eat. I do not want to send them away hungry, or they may collapse on the way." Jesus' disciples began to think about the money it would cost to feed the crowd of people gathered. Then Jesus said to them, "You give them something to eat" (Mark 6:37).

Jesus was attentive to the needs of people who were looking for solutions, were hungry or sick, among others. At the end of the parable of the good Samaritan Jesus asked the Scribe whom he thought was the compassionate neighbor, and when the scribe pointed out that it was the Samaritan, Jesus said to him, "Go and do likewise" (Luke 10:37).

# WHO SHOULD GET INVOLVED IN SERVING OUR NEIGHBORS?

In fact, all Christians must collaborate in the ministries of the church, even those of service to the neighbor. The book of Acts teaches us that early Christians developed diverse ministries in the church to meet the different needs of the people in their community. Some things these Christians did together were:

1. They had fellowship with one another.
2. They were studying the Word of God together.
3. They prayed together.
4. They maintained the doctrine of the Apostles.
5. They met the material needs of the neediest members.

It is important to clarify here that serving others is not easy. Many times even in the midst of our best intentions we encounter difficulties. This happened in the Church of the book of Acts. The apostles soon realized that they could not do everything.

The apostles asked that the church select brethren who could coordinate the task of aid for the needy as this was important. They searched for people with some special characteristics to fulfill this task:

**1. Be a good witness**, that is, be a good example to others. These should be members of the church who also knew and understood the problems of the people of their community.

**2. Full of the Holy Spirit**, since the Holy Spirit helps us to see people in need from God's perspective.

**3. Wise people** with the capacity to respond to the problems of the needy and to help them in the best way possible.

It is the presence of the Spirit of God that enables believers to use their abilities and intelligence to serve others. It is a privilege for every child of God to be able to serve others, especially in their human needs. Through this service, those in difficulty can see God acting through us in love to bring relief to their needs.

# HOW CAN WE CONTRIBUTE TO A MINISTRY OF SERVICE IN THE CHURCH?

Initially, we must know that each of us can be instrumental in collaborating in a ministry of service in our church.

For this, we can begin by identifying the abilities and talents that we have, and receive training for this type of ministry. If there is already a ministry in our church, we can contact the leaders and offer our help. If it is not yet organized, we can make a suggestion to the pastor about starting one. In the latter case, we can involve other members of the church to work in this ministry. Some will have a God given 'gift of service'[4] who will be the pillars on which this ministry rests.

There are three basic steps to keep in mind when planning service ministries:

### 1. Identification of the need.

The first thing to do is to identify well the needs of people. Assuming a misconception of a necessity will lead us to give a wrong answer.

### 2. Identification of Resources.

We must identify the resources available to help people. What financial and people resource does the church have to use to help? God always multiplies resources. If we do our part, God will do the rest.

### 3. Planning activities.

Planning is basic to everything we do, even when we want to help people. Planning is the secret of success if we can develop it all according to plan. Let us not forget that when we want to help people, we must pray and wait on the Lord as if everything depended on Him, and then we have to make every effort as if everything depended on us.

# WHO SHOULD BENEFIT FROM A SERVICE PROGRAM?

Because there is much need in our world, we often find it difficult to choose who to help and we ask ourselves, who really needs help? How should we select the people we can and should help?

The Bible guides us in this regard by offering us an example of people we can help with some advice on how to do it:

## 1. Widows.

Widows and widowers are people who are going through difficult situations, adjusting to a new way of life. It is a stage where they need a lot of help in many ways.

In Exodus 22:22 we are told, "Do not take advantage of the widow ..." That is, we must not increase their suffering, putting loads on them that they are not fit to carry.

In Psalm 146:9 we read that the Lord "sustains the fatherless and the widow." This is an invitation to us to support them in all their needs.

The apostle Paul says in Titus 2:3 that we should honor the true widows who really are, those who are truly in need.

In James 1:27 we read an interesting statement, "Religion that God our Father accepts as pure and faultless is this, to look after orphans and widows in their distress and to keep oneself from being polluted by the world."

This brings us to another group of people where we can focus our help plans:

## 2. Orphans.

Orphans are children whom life's circumstances have left them without one or both parents. Life for them is extremely difficult. They need the help of Christians to get ahead in life. Let's look again at what the Bible says about this.

Deuteronomy 10:18 says that God, "defends the cause of the fatherless and the widow..., giving them food and clothing."

Psalm 82:3 is more direct. It tells us to "Defend the weak and the fatherless; uphold the cause of the poor and the oppressed." Who is weaker than an orphan child?

The prophet Isaiah in his book also refers to the needs of the orphans: "Learn to do right; seek justice."

"Defend the oppressed. Take up the cause of the fatherless; plead the case of the widow"(1:17).

God is always interested in the weakest, the neediest. Is there anyone more needy and abandoned than an orphan child?

Let us advance in our group of potential beneficiaries of our compassion. In the Old Testament another group is mentioned together with widows and orphans, whom we also want to refer to.

## 3. Foreigners

How did you feel when you visit a place for the first time, whether it's a church, a village, a school, or some other place unknown to you? Always the first experience is difficult. We feel bad, different; we think everyone looks at us. That is also the feeling of a stranger.

God said, "Do not mistreat or oppress a foreigner" (Exodus 22:21). Foreigners must occupy a special place in our hearts.

In Leviticus 23:22, God counsels his people not to harvest to the last corner of the field but to leave something for the poor and foreigners. We could say that today we must deal with the material needs of foreigners and the poor as well.

In Deuteronomy 10:19, God told his people, "you are to love those who are foreigners." We ourselves could be in that situation at some point in our life and we would want to be loved.

The prophet Jeremiah is quite emphatic. God said, "Do what is just and right. Rescue from the hand of the oppressor the one who has been robbed. Do no wrong or violence to the foreigner, the fatherless or the widow, and do not shed innocent blood in this place" (22:3).

These are three very important groups of people that we must take into account when asking ourselves: Whom should I help? But we must still consider other groups of the needy that we could find in our surroundings. We must have our eyes and ears attentive to see the needs that God sees in our community.

# WHAT SHOULD WE DO TO HELP THOSE IN NEED?

This is another question that we should consider. How can we help? What can we give? What can we do?

In a biblical passage about how God will judge the nations, we find the following teaching (Matthew 25:31-46).

Verses 31-40 states:

"When the Son of Man comes in his glory, and all the angels with him, he will sit on his glorious throne. All the nations will be gathered before him, and he will separate the people one from another as a shepherd separates the sheep from the goats. He will put the sheep on his right and the goats on his left. Then the King will say to those on his right, 'Come, you who are blessed by my Father; take your inheritance, the kingdom prepared for you since the creation of the world. For I was hungry and you gave me something to eat, I was thirsty and you gave me something to drink, I was a stranger and you invited me in, I needed clothes and you clothed me, I was sick and you looked after me, I was in prison and you came to visit me.' "Then the righteous will answer him, 'Lord, when did we see you hungry and feed you, or thirsty and give you something to drink? When did we see you a stranger and invite you in, or needing clothes and clothe you? When did we see you sick or in prison and go to visit you?' "The King will reply, 'Truly I tell you, whatever you did for one of the least of these brothers and sisters of mine, you did for me.'"

What do you think of this scene? Apart from the drama of how the Lord will judge our actions, it also provides us with a list of ways in which we can help those in need, whether individually, as a group, or as part of the Church's work to which we belong.

Let's look at the list.

## HUNGER

Hunger is one of the most serious problems for the human being. When children still cannot speak, they cry to indicate they are hungry. In Latin America and the Caribbean today, many children are suffering from malnutrition due to lack of food (in some countries up to 60% of children under five years of age). What can Christians do so that the Lord can say to us, "I was hungry and you fed me"?

The Bible tells us about many people who suffered from hunger in history. In Isaiah 58:7, it says that God is pleased that his children voluntarily abstain from food to share their bread with the hungry.

How many people around us are hungry? We can be the

solution to the hunger of these people if we share what we have with them, especially the children, the elderly, the disabled, etc. But we can go further in our action to alleviate hunger.

Many people are hungry because they do not have work. We could help them to find work so that they could satisfy their needs without creating dependency. We could help them receive training in order to have better possibilities of work to improve their economic income.

Day care centers and children's feeding centers in churches are another way of responding to the need for food in the community. Church-based nutrition programs are very successful in combating the problem of hunger.

In agricultural areas, we could provide training courses for farmers that result in better harvests, or switch to producing other products that can improve their standard of living and satisfy their need for food.

So we can see that our response can range from sharing bread with the hungry to getting involved in social development programs that improve people's economic capacity. The Lord Jesus will tell you, "Whatever you did for one of the least of these brothers and sisters of mine, you did for me" (Matthew 25:40).

## THIRST

Another major problem of humanity today is the lack of drinkable water. How hard it is to be thirsty, to have need of water, and to know that there is none!

Remember the story of the people of Israel in the desert when they were willing to start a rebellion against Moses because of the lack of water? They said to him, "You brought us into this desert to die of thirst." God provided water from a rock and gave them plenty of water.

In the Gospel of Matthew 10:42, it says, "And if anyone gives even a cup of cold water to one of these little ones who is my disciple, truly I tell you, that person will certainly not lose their reward."

We can settle for simply giving a "glass" of water to the thirsty, but meeting the water needs of some communities could imply finding a permanent solution that will really solve their problem permanently.

It is also important to teach communities to conserve pure water sources. One of the problems of today's world is environmental destruction. The destruction of forests is causing the loss of important sources of natural water. Environmental pollution is transforming pure water sources into water unfit for human consumption.

The Bible tells a story of the prophet Elisha. Once they came to tell him that the water was bad for the people. He asked for a new vessel and salt and with it purified the water (2 Kings 2:19-22). Could we also get involved as individuals and as a church to obtain good quality water for our neighbors? One way would be to get involved in neighborhood committees to improve the community's access to water.

## THE POORLY CLOTHED

The situation of poverty and isolation makes many people today lack appropriate clothing. In isolated communities where there is extreme poverty, people have scarcely enough to survive. At some times of the year, especially the very cold times, people need extra clothing or blankets to cover themselves, otherwise they might become sick or even die from lack of shelter.

When there are natural disasters like floods, earthquakes, hurricanes, people lose all their things, including their clothes.

What are we willing to do? John the Baptist preached in the time of Jesus. On one occasion he spoke to his audience about the needs of the people. Those who listened to him then asked him, "What can we do?" He gave them an interesting answer: "Anyone who has two shirts should share with the one who has none, and anyone who has food should do the same" (Luke 3:11). We could say today, "Whoever has more clothes than they need should really share them with those who do not have enough." They should be clothes in good condition, something that we ourselves would wear.

The Apostle James reminds us in his letter: "Suppose a brother or a sister is without clothes and daily food. If one of you says to them, 'Go in peace; keep warm and well fed,' but does nothing about their physical needs, what good is it?" (2:15-16). Clothing and footwear can be very useful to people in need; we must share what we have.

## DISEASE

"I was sick and you visited me." The loneliness of the sick is terrible. When a person is sick, a visitor, prayer, and comfort is a great help even in the recovery process.

The Bible urges us to pray for the sick and to visit them. The book of James says that the prayer of faith will heal the sick. Some scientific studies are now discovering that this is a great truth. In biblical times, visiting the sick was the only thing that could be done for him. In our time, situations have changed; we can do much more for them. What do you think we can do for the sick besides visiting, praying, and anointing with oil?

I would like to give some suggestions in this direction:

1.  We could go and help clean the house and support the other members of the family, especially if the patient is the mother.

2.  We could go and help with the purchase of medicines needed for recovery. Many times disease aggravates the family's economic situation and they cannot afford to buy medicines that would help them to get better faster.

3.  We could take the patient to the doctor, to a private or public clinic; sometimes the patient does not know where to go, or his illness does not allow him to seek help. Sometimes this will also mean that we may have to support financially with the expenses.

4.  In some churches, there are medical professionals who could donate their time to start health care programs in the church, using the facilities that the church already has, such as its annexes, Sunday school classrooms, etc. This will help people come with confidence and without having the problem of facing the health care costs that are now truly high.

Just as we can do much more than just visit the patient, we can also deal with searching for solutions to the problem of disease. There are communities where there is a chronic health problem, depending on how folks live. We could be part of a church program initiating health education programs so that people do not get sick. If we use the Bible as a health manual, we will find great truths that teach people to live according to the principles of God's Word.

We often repeat that "God is our Healer," but we forget the conditions for healing. In Exodus 15:26, we find this passage: "If you listen carefully to the Lord your God and do what is right in his eyes, if you pay attention to his commands and keep all his decrees, I will not bring on you any of the diseases I brought on the Egyptians, for I am the Lord, who heals you." If we teach the commandments of God to all, we could contribute to removing some of the diseases that harass communities.

## PRISONERS

Those who are in prison are possibly the most difficult people to minister to, but they are also the most needy.

The prophet Isaiah, inspired by the Spirit of God, spoke these words about the work that Jesus would do in the world: "The Spirit of the Sovereign Lord is on me, because the Lord has anointed me to proclaim good news to the poor. He has sent me to bind up the brokenhearted, to proclaim freedom for the captives and release from darkness for the prisoners" (Isaiah 61:1).

The task involves more than just visiting the prisoners; we must seek how to free them. Especially to help them find freedom from the power of sin through a personal encounter with Jesus Christ, and to disciple them to live as Christians while they are still in prison.

Prisoners are exposed to many problems, even to learn more perversities. Many get out of jail even worse than when they went in, and eventually return to prison. How can Christians help in the rehabilitation of prisoners?

We could start by visiting them in prison. This can be difficult if we do not know each other very well. Many churches hold services in the prisons. We can do even more than this. Prisoners need to learn how to live in dignity within the prison. We could help them through programs of study, training for work, etc. So that when they leave the prison, they will be able to fit into society and will not just return to commit crimes.

We need to remember too that the family of the prisoner may well be going through times of great need because there is no one who generates sufficient income. We can be of help to them by visiting and assisting them according to their needs.

Another important issue to consider is the rehabilitation process when they leave the prison. It is very difficult for a former prisoner to join society if he does not have a helping hand, to help find work and get used to living in freedom again.

What do you think of these varied ways in which we can serve others and at the same time demonstrate Christian character? There is plenty for us to do. Christian compassion is a way we can demonstrate in concrete actions the change that God has made in our lives.

# BASIC ELEMENTS OF COMPASSION

It is possible that after reading all this you are asking yourself, Can I put compassion into practice in my life? Will I be able to help my neighbor? Let me tell you that all the children of God have the potential to love others compassionately and serve them accordingly.

The story of the good Samaritan in Luke 10:25-37 mentions three elements that must be present in every action of helping others that we undertake.

**1. LOVE:** This is the most important ingredient of a help program. The apostle Paul in 1 Corinthians 13:3 says that even if we distribute all we have to feed the poor, even give our body to be burned, but do it without love, it's useless. Love is the most important necessity in the world today. All of us who have accepted Christ as our Savior have received an inheritance of love from Him and can share it with others. People are eager to see and receive the love of God.

**2. TIME:** In the story of the Samaritan, we can see that he invested at least one day and one night helping this man who was a stranger. Jesus always took time to help the needy. Why is it so difficult for us to spend time for others? We must always remember that Jesus gave us time when we were lost and without hope of salvation. We must give time to those who need our help.

**3. OUR OWN RESOURCES:** The Samaritan invested his own resources in helping this wounded traveler. He cleaned his wounds and then brought him to the inn and paid for the expenses. An aid program needs us to investment our resources.

Here we have these three elements of compassion: love, time and money. Sharing them many times will demand sacrifice, it will not be easy. The question for us today is: Are we willing to follow the example of Jesus? Jesus' command continues, "Go and do likewise" (Luke 10:37).

## REFERENCE

(1) Redeemer: comes from the verb "to redeem" which means to buy with a price something that was lost. Out of love God paid the price of our freedom from the dominion of sin by giving His Son Jesus to die on the cross in our place.

(2) Manna: substance produced by some plants similar to cotton candy that God provided abundantly and miraculously for 40 years while the people of Israel were living in the wilderness of Sinai (Exodus 16:35).

(3) Quail: a bird similar in size to a small hen that moves in groups. God also provided enough of these birds to the people of Israel in the wilderness of Sinai (Exodus 16:13).

(4) Gifts of service: Gifts are given by God to His children, such as salvation, love, and others. God also enables His children to do certain ministries or works for Him. This ability comes from God and is perfected through study and practice. The gifts of service mentioned here are those that relate to the capacities and talents that a person needs to serve the needs of others, such as: being kind and hospitable; being willing to perform tasks such as caring for the sick, caring for children, the elderly; also people with ability to prepare food, to sew clothes, to clean, to heal, to give advice, among others.

# HISTORY AND MINISTRY OF THE CHURCH OF THE NAZARENE IN THE WORLD

**Ruthie Córdova Carvallo**

## INTRODUCTION

The Church of the Nazarene emerged within a context of spiritual awakening in the United States through the preaching and teaching of the biblical doctrine of holiness. A century earlier in England, there was also a revival of holiness led by the preacher John Wesley.

18th-century England at the time of John Wesley saw the beginning of the Industrial Revolution, It was a time when some people were very wealthy, but the poor were getting poorer. Many people were moving to the new cities which were dirty, noisy, and overcrowded. The Anglican Church neglected biblical teachings, and the clergy did not receive proper theological studies and were more interested in maintaining their ecclesiastical positions.

In the midst of this situation, some faithful Christians sought ways to change the country, seeking to improve the moral condition of the people with the support of the government, creating societies to reform customs and set up centers of religious life. In this context, John Wesley received his education, and prepared to be a clergyman. His own spiritual experience and communion with God were the foundations of many of the decisions he took in his life and ministry. He became a key instrument of God in teaching the doctrine of holiness, proclaiming it and living it out in the midst of a society in crisis.

Wesley worked hard among the needy, struggling against injustice and evil. He was concerned about people's social needs as well as their spiritual growth. His fervent desire was that all should come to know God in a personal way and learn to obey the Bible. He made an effort to train his preachers both theologically and above all inspiring them to have a passion to proclaim the good news of salvation.

Throughout the kingdom the revival spread. Many people came to listen to Wesley's preaching, and many of them repented of their sinful lives. It affected not only the spiritual life of the country but also brought about some reforms which improved aspects of social justice. The responses were so numerous that Wesley was forced to organize a movement, and Methodism was born. With a fervent missionary vision, they took the newly founded denomination to the United States.

# Holiness Movement in the USA

The great revival[1] under John Wesley was taken to the British colonies in North America by Thomas Webb, who started to preach the doctrine of Christian perfection[2] in this new nation. He was joined by another young English preacher Francis Asbury, and together they established numerous meeting places where the Bible was preached.

Methodism[3] began to grow little by little in North America, but at the same time, Christians of the Pietism movement[4] arrived from different European countries, influencing the thinking and ways of the people. The preaching of the gospel and the doctrine of holiness was heard everywhere. Little by little, people began to understand the different aspects of this experience. Lay people of different churches congregated in houses every week to do Bible studies and to preach the doctrine of Christian perfection. Teaching about sanctification was emphasized, including how to live the life of holiness and how to witness to others by sharing their own experiences.

During these meetings, which were attended not only by Methodists but by Christians of other denominations, many people were inspired to seek holiness of heart while evangelists and preachers talked of spiritual renewal. Men and women who obtained the experience of holiness, proclaimed it strongly and by example. The revival of holiness spread throughout the country. Prayer crusades, home meetings, publications, open-air type meetings, (among others) were held, with the sole purpose of preaching and promoting the doctrine of holiness. For a long time, there was great spiritual renewal, but it was impeded by the outburst of the Civil War in the United

States between the Northern and Southern States.

Later, tensions arose in the church with respect to the most acceptable forms of conduct and of adoration. In order to revive the churches, camp meetings were held to promote holiness, but this created new tensions between the church as an established institution and open air meetings during the week, fostering controversies.

To this was added the appearance of preachers who proposed reforms but who brought about divisions. Proponents of the doctrine of holiness formed a group called the "Holiness Movement." Later, opponents of the doctrine caused the movement to fragment in such a way that 23 different holiness denominations were formed in only seven years.

## Biography of Phineas F. Bresee

Phineas Franklin Bresee was born on December 31, 1838 in a rustic cottage in Franklin Village, Delaware County in the state of New York. Phineas was the second of three children. His parents were Phineas P. Bresee, owner of a farm and a store, and his wife Susana, both Christians and members of the Methodist Episcopal Church.

Phineas studied his elementary and secondary education in New York but was unable to pursue higher education due to lack of financial resources. Although he had grown up in a Christian home, at 18 years of age, he accepted Jesus as his personal Savior. One year later he was called into the pastoral ministry. So the Methodist Episcopal Church appointed him as associate pastor for one year with the Rev. A. C. Barnhart. With his help, Phineas took and passed all his ministerial courses. The following year, he was given the pastorate of a jurisdiction in Pella, Iowa and after a year, when Phineas was 21, he was granted his first pastoral license. He believed in education and was able to emphasize this aspect in his ministerial life, in the preparation of other ministries and in the new denomination.

Phineas was considered a trusted leader as he was very active and committed to missionary work. He became a strong preacher of Christian life and character, as he would be later of the doctrine and life of holiness. He had a compassionate heart; being sensitive to the needs of others, Phineas visited the needy and sick, bringing them food and money from his own resources. He had a passion for the evangelization of the poor and the proclamation of the life of holiness. Likewise, he opposed in words and deeds social inequality, and fought in campaigns against alcohol.

In addition to all this, Phineas F. Bresee was a young man with vision. Each church that he pastored grew and became a center of revival where the message of the gospel and the doctrine of holiness were clearly preached; moreover he practiced what he preached.

Two years later in 1861, Phineas Bresee was ordained as a pastor and returned to New York to marry his girlfriend Mary Hibbard. During those years, slavery was in force. Phineas did not support slavery which was very strong in the South. Therefore, he requested a change from Pella, Iowa to another jurisdiction. He was then assigned to Galesburg, also in Iowa. It was a fairly difficult area. For some time, Bresee was frustrated and bitter about the place, but after praying much, he took it as a challenge and asked God to help him.

Within a year of pastoring in that area, Bresee received 140 new members in his church. He could buy a comfortable pastoral house, two horses and carriage. Phineas Bresee was now 23 years old and had demonstrated perseverance and success in his ministry as a pastor. He was then assigned to pastor a good church in Des Moines, the capital of Iowa. He would go on to save the church from financial ruin.

At age 28, Phineas Bresee received the experience of entire sanctification after a time of searching for answers to his questions and doubts about the Christian faith. Above all, because he realized that in his life there were tendencies to anger, pride and material ambition that he did not want to have. This event took place at one of his local church's prayer meetings when he prayed, asking God for the experience that would cleanse those tendencies from his life.

Over the years, Bresee grew in his spiritual life and developed his ministry pastoring several churches, both small and large, in the countryside as well as in cities, in different States, assuming numerous important positions of leadership in the denomination.

When he was 45, he was sent to preach at the First Methodist Episcopal Church in Los Angeles, California. The congregation liked him so much that within two weeks of being there, he was asked to be their pastor.

Then in 1886, he was invited to pastor a small church in a small neighborhood in Pasadena, California. Bresee accepted and started open-air evangelistic campaigns and meetings with the construction workers who lived there. From here on, a series of events occurred that would make Phineas begin to develop the vision of an international church of holiness.

Bresee's ministry was very dynamic and varied. He did not settle in a local church but traveled about promoting holiness. From age 57 onwards, Phineas F. Bresee would initiate a denomination of holiness and live to see the fruits, outreach, ministries and preachers that came out of it. He continued to preach holiness until the last year of his life. He died when he was 77 years old on November 13, 1915.

## Origins of the Church of the Nazarene

In 1895, when Bresee was 57, he began to leave the pulpits of Methodism to minister to the poor. His desire was to have a workers' organization that allowed non-churchgoers to be part of the mission that he wanted to create and be considered as their spiritual home. While he was pastoring, Bresee managed to rent a building in the city of Peniel in California, and he began his work of evangelization among construction and factory workers. This ministry was called the Peniel Mission. He asked for his leader's approval to work there full time, which implied giving up the pastorate of the local church. They agreed, but were not happy to maintain this independent work. As a result, Bresee remained a Methodist minister, but without the support of a local church. The owners of the rented property asked him to leave as they felt that it was not a very prosperous venture. Phineas Bresee was very sad and disconcerted as almost all the ministry had to stop. With much soul searching and after much prayer, Bresee asked his leaders to put his name on the list of inactive ministers in the denomination.

In those days, Bresee learned that his good friend Dr. Widney was back in the city after pursuing some secular studies. They met together, and after sharing and praying together, they decided to form a new organization to continue the program of providing a spiritual home for the poor. With the help of several friends, they managed to get a much larger room to rent and the group moved in. After the first services, they could see that the work was going to grow, so they decided to organize themselves as a church. Their first official meeting was on October 6, 1895 in Red Men's Hall, near Peniel, California. Two weeks later, they had a congregation of 86 including the families of leading Methodist friends and as well as their own families. This initial group was organized as the Church of the Nazarene.

In the opening service, Dr. Widney preached a message based on Luke's gospel on Jesus' words to his disciples "follow me". In his message, Widney explained that the reason for founding a new denomination was that the methods and administration of the older church had been an obstacle to the work of evangelization of the poor. He also said that the name of the Church of the Nazarene was chosen because it seemed to him that the word "Nazarene" symbolized the humble and laborious mission of Jesus. It was also the name that Jesus himself used and that his enemies used to mock him.

Faced with continuous growth, Bresee prayed for the possibility of obtaining land to build a larger church. Months later, God provided that place, and they built a church building with the capacity for 400 people. The congregation continued to grow so they had to think about expanding the building to receive 600 people.

The services of worship and holiness preaching attracted more and more people.

Many were converted and many were sanctified; the revival was incredible. The Nazarenes showed their joy in singing, as well as their devotion to and understanding of the experience of holiness as the truths of the Bible which they had been taught. Very soon, people from all over the US and even other denominations came to this Church of the Nazarene in Los Angeles, California. After this, they opened other churches in nearby towns, and later the work spread to neighboring States. In 1897, the Church of the Nazarene was interested in preaching to other cultures, so they established a mission among Hispanics in Los Angeles, California, which spread to Texas and a mission among the Chinese community.

In the following years, the growth of the Church of the Nazarene and other churches of holiness in the country was such that they began to unite to share efforts and promote the work. The Rhode Island Evangelical People's Church teamed up with the Independent Holiness Church of Massachusetts. The Central Evangelical Holiness Association joined the Pentecostal Churches Association of North America. The New Testament Church of Christ united with the Independent Church of Holiness. On October 11, 1907, in Chicago, the Association of Pentecostal Churches of North America united with the Church of the Nazarene resulting in the Church of the Pentecostal Nazarene.

In the General Assembly, Rev. H.F. Reynolds joined Phineas F. Bresee, as General Superintendents. On October 13, 1908 in Pilot Point, Texas, the Church of Christ of Holiness was united with the Pentecostal Nazarene Church and Rev. E.P. Ellyson was added as another General Superintendent. In February 1915, the Pentecostal Holiness Mission joined the Church of the Nazarene Pentecostal. Other holiness groups joined the Church of the Nazarene later. Their agreement of union was based on the basic doctrines of the Christian life and what was essential to holiness.

In the General Assembly of 1919 at the request of the Districts, the word "Pentecostal" was taken from the name of the denomination because in the religious sphere, the word "Pentecostal" had come to mean speaking in tongues. Some denominations promoted this gift and the word created some confusion among the people who thought that the Church of the Nazarene was one of them. Therefore, the official name of the denomination returned to its original form, the "Church of the Nazarene."

## Policy, Structure and Growth

The Church of the Nazarene from the beginning emphasized evangelism, education and compassion as areas of ministry. As the denomination grew and impacted the world, other areas of ministry and programs were added and promoted in order to minister to people in their entirety.

Thus, several Committees and the General Board were formed to represent the ministries of the denomination. Among them were committees of missions, church growth, social assistance, publications, education, ministry and others. These committees were then consolidated into General Boards and various departments.

The General Budget was established which would be collected from the offerings of local churches and districts; the funds would be divided among the departments or ministries of the church. This is now called the World Evangelism Fund. Years later, the denomination restructured the organization and created divisions and departments such as the Sunday School Ministries Division, Church Growth Division, Finance Division, Communications Division and Global Mission Division.

At the 1976 General Assembly, an internationalization commission was created with the purpose of becoming an international community and promoting national leadership. Thus, in the 1980 General Assembly, a system of world regions was created and divided the church into regions and fields. Currently the church is divided into six world regions - Mesoamerica (Mexico, Central America, and the Caribbean), South America, USA & Canada, Eurasia, Asia Pacific, and Africa.

The General Assembly is the highest decision-making body of the whole organization of the denomination. Any action, decision, modification, elimination, etc. of an Article of Faith (beliefs), or changes to the structures of government must be approved or rejected by this global assembly of delegates. The General Assembly nominates the Board of General Superintendents (consisting of six ordained ministers).

Since the organization of the Church of the Nazarene, the publication of a Manual, which states beliefs, the form of government and the organization, general rules and rituals, has been developed until today. This manual is continually being updated to keep up with changes in society, different cultures and countries where the church is, circumstances and specific cases, confrontation or currents of thought, among others.

Every change in the Manual is carefully studied and evaluated in order to be faithful to the Scriptures, the Wesleyan-Arminian theological tradition,[5] in keeping with the founders of the denomination, the cultural sensitivity and the present times. Each change is presented, discussed, reviewed, endorsed and accepted by delegate members from all countries at each General Assembly.

Today, the Church of the Nazarene continues to proclaim the message of salvation and Holiness to nations making a difference in the lives of many people through their various ministries in the world. In the 2017 statistical report, the total membership was 2,550,374. The education institutions are located in 35 countries on six continents and serve a richly diverse student body offering phenomenal opportunities for the more than 50,000 students who annually make Nazarene institutions their schools of choice. The World Evangelism Fund was created to allow missionaries to work more effectively and to encourage all churches to support missions. The World Evangelism Fund goes directly toward accomplishing the mission of the Church of the Nazarene, to make Christlike disciples in the nations. The World Evangelism Fund provides the funds needed to operate the Church of the Nazarene and its entire mission effort, from the church's Global Ministry to the districts and churches around the world.

# MISSION OF THE CHURCH OF The NAZARENE

We are a Great Commission church (Matthew 28:19-20). As a global community of faith, we are commissioned to take the Good News of life in Jesus Christ to people everywhere and to spread the message of scriptural holiness (Christlike living) across the lands.

The Church of the Nazarene bonds together individuals who have made Jesus Christ Lord of their lives, sharing in Christian fellowship, and seeking to strengthen each other in faith development through worship, preaching, training, and service to others.

We strive to express the compassion of Jesus Christ to all persons along with our personal commitment to Christlike living. While the primary motive of the church is to glorify God, we also are called to actively participate in His mission—reconciling the world to himself.

The statement of mission contains historical essentials of our mission: evangelism, sanctification, discipleship, compassion. The essence of holiness is Christlikeness. Nazarenes are becoming a sent people—into homes, work places, communities, and villages as well as other cities and countries. Missionaries are now sent from all regions of the world. God continues calling ordinary people to do extraordinary things made possible by the person of the Holy Spirit.

# CORE VALUES

## a) We are a Christian people

As members of the Church Universal, we join with all true believers in proclaiming the Lordship of Jesus Christ and in affirming the historic Trinitarian creeds and beliefs of the Christian faith. We value our Wesleyan-Holiness heritage and believe it to be a way of understanding the faith that is true to Scripture, reason, tradition, and experience.

## b) We are a holiness people

God, who is holy, calls us to a life of holiness. We believe that the Holy Spirit seeks to do in us a second work of grace, called by various terms including "entire sanctification" and "baptism with the Holy Spirit" - cleansing us from all sin, renewing us in the image of God, empowering us to love God with our whole heart, soul, mind, and strength, and our neighbors as ourselves, and producing in us the character of Christ. Holiness in the life of believers is most clearly understood as Christlikeness.

## c) We are a missional people

We are a sent people, responding to the call of Christ and empowered by the Holy Spirit to go into all the world, witnessing to the Lordship of Christ and participating with God in the building of the Church and the extension of His kingdom (Matthew 28:19-20; 2 Corinthians 6:1). Our mission:

1. begins in worship,
2. ministers to the world in evangelism and compassion,
3. encourages believers toward Christian maturity through discipleship, and
4. prepares women and men for Christian service through Christian higher education.

# REFERENCES

1. Revival: Deep spiritual awakening realized by God in the lives of people.

2. Christian Perfection: Doctrine of the complete salvation of sin and the fullness of the Christian life realized by God over believers. Also known as "entire sanctification."

3. Methodism: Evangelical group founded by John Wesley. Its name comes from the methodical, the devotion of its members for the service to the needy, among others

4. Pietista: Movement of spiritual renovation of century XVII. It is known as the religion of the heart.

5. Arminian: Protestant theological current taught by Jacobo Arminio (16th and 17th century). Wesley resumed and expanded the Arminian line of thought.

# BIBLIOGRAPHY

Du Bois, Layriston J., Guidelines for Conduct.

Dunn, Samuel L., Opportunity Unlimited.

Hamlin, Howard H., Let's Look at Our Church.

Johnson, Jerald D., The International Experience.

Taylor, Mendell, Handbook of Historical Documents of the Church of the Nazarene, thesis. Kansas City, sf.

Metz, Donald S., Some Crucial Issues in the Church of the Nazarene. Wesleyan Heritage Press, 1994.

Purkiser, W.T., Called Unto Holiness. Vol II.

Price, Ross E., Nazarene Manifesto.

Redford, M.E., Rise of the Church of the Nazarene

Smith, Timothy L., The Story of the Nazarenes - The Formative Years, Vol. I. Kansas City

Young, Bill. Sucedió en un pueblito. Kansas City: Casa Nazarena de Publicaciones, sf.

Manual of the Church of the Nazarene.

# HOW SHOULD A SPIRIT-FILLED CHRISTIAN LIVE

**Ulises Daniel Solís**

## INTRODUCTION:

One of the many benefits of being a Christian is the blessed privilege given by Jesus Christ to live free from all sin and experience joy in the midst of a world where there is much evil and suffering.

The holy life is a joyful life which is a product of the Christian experience of giving all of our being to the Lord and of being freed from selfishness (also called the old man). This is a very intimate and real experience that is not altered even when we are in the midst of the biggest storms of daily life. This joy is the product of a new relationship that the Christian enjoys with Christ and of being filled with the power of the Holy Spirit (Ephesians 4:17-24).

Of course, being filled with the Holy Spirit of God is the greatest honor and privilege a human being can enjoy in this life. However, it should be kept in mind that every privilege is accompanied by commitment and responsibility. It is about some of these responsibilities and privileges for daily life, shared by the members of the Church of the Nazarene around the world, which we will discuss below.

## CHRISTIAN LIFE IS DIFFERENT

In the first place, all Christians who belong to the family of God must be aware that the divine presence dwells in their being through the Holy Spirit (1 Corinthians 6:19-20).

This Spirit of God dwelling in believers is "holy." This implies that true Christians should turn away from every sinful word, thought or action, since those corrupt their genuine relationship with God (1 Corinthians 15:33, 2 Corinthians 6:14-18). Every authentic disciple of Jesus Christ must always follow His example. Jesus willingly obeyed his Father and sought to please him in everything, and this is the same thing that Jesus expects of all his followers (Matthew 16:24, Luke 22:42).

Secondly, the new believer filled with the Spirit of God must live a holy life, but should not do so as a burden or obligation. It is a privilege to live in holiness, even in the midst of a postmodern culture that is intentionally ignoring the ethical principles and values that God has given us in His Word. Only children who live in holiness can serve a God who is holy (1 Peter 1:16).

# WHAT ARE CHRISTIAN ETHICS?

Ethics is that branch of philosophical science whose interest is to determine what is good and right. Christian ethics is a specialized branch of ethics that seeks to find answers in the Bible. Christian ethics helps us to know what our duties are to God, to ourselves and to others. Its ethical norms guide us for our good and for the benefit of others.

One of the biblical sections summarizing God's ethical demands for human beings is the Ten Commandments that Moses received on Mount Sinai for the people of Israel (Exodus 20:3-17). These Ten Commandments provide a very valuable guide to help believers live in holiness with God and our fellow human beings.

Spirit-filled believers must model their lives on Jesus who taught us an ethical standard that sums up all others: "So in everything, do to others what you would have them do to you, for this sums up the Law and the Prophets" (Matthew 7:12). If all Christians in the world obeyed this standard of Christian ethics one hundred percent, many of the problems that afflict our churches and our communities would end.

What are some of the ethical behaviors that identify Nazarene Christians?

a. Their lives represent people in whom the Spirit of God dwells and therefore present the characteristics that distinguish the family of God.

b. They attend regularly services in the Church of the Nazarene and voluntarily engage in the church's ministries as a product of their gratitude and the divine presence in their hearts (Acts 1:8).

c. Their lifestyle will reflect holiness. There should be a decisive break with all sinful practice because their inner purity rejects them (John 17:14).

d. They seek to relate to other Christians to worship God or to perform any other good work to benefit the community.

# CHRISTIAN LIFE IMPLIES SHARING IN THE COMMUNITY OF FAITH

In the Bible we find concrete guidelines to reaffirm our faith in Christ which produce trust and peace for our daily lives; we find beautiful recommendations like the following:

"Let us hold unswervingly to the hope we profess, for he who promised is faithful. And let us consider how we may spur one another on toward love and good deeds, not giving up meeting together, as some are in the habit of doing, but encouraging one another—and all the more as you see the Day approaching" ( Hebrews 10:23-25).

In the local church, we have the opportunity to give support to others and to find brothers and sisters full of love that will encourage us to continue in the midst of social and economic pressures. In the local congregation, we find pastoral care and the opportunity to serve and perform Christian ministry. In addition, we can find teaching of the Word where Jesus comforts us and encourages us to persevere in the Christian faith. Let's look at some examples of these passages:

- "Do not be afraid, little flock, for your Father has been pleased to give you the kingdom" (Luke 12:32).

- "Do not let your hearts be troubled. You believe in God; believe also in me" (John 14:1).

- "Peace I leave with you; my peace I give you. I do not give to you as the world gives. Do not let your hearts be troubled and do not be afraid" (John 14:27).

Early Christians gathered on the first day of the week (Sunday) to pray and study the teachings of Christ (Acts 2:42). They experienced the joy of being saved from sin. This joy they displayed outwardly as a testimony to the inner joy that the Spirit had given them. Therefore, if you are a Christian who enjoys the blessing of being filled with the Spirit, share joyfully and proclaim the gospel and Christian holiness in an appealing way, because a sad Christian will remain sterile and fruitless.

In addition to reflecting a good testimony to everyone, Christians must also be an example of conduct in all areas of life.

# CHRISTIANS AVOID HARMFUL PRACTICES AND CUSTOMS

Every believer full of the spirit is called to be governed by three principles:

a. The Christian stewardship of free time. We are Christians always and everywhere. Members of the Church of the Nazarene around the world have agreed to live out the biblical principle of living a balanced life in our free time. For this we must avoid activities that directly or indirectly lead or promote sin and evil. Examples of these are: playing the lottery or betting of any kind, consumption or sale of alcoholic beverages and drugs, attending concerts and dance halls where a sinful life is promoted, watching movies or reading books or magazines or indecent websites as well as attending meetings that promote a sinful way of living, among others (1 Corinthians 6:12, 10:23, 31, 1 Thessalonians 5:21-22, 1 Timothy 6:6-11).

b. To apply the highest moral norms of the Christian life when selecting entertainments for us and our family. Because we live in days of great moral confusion, subtle forms of evil and sin are introduced into our homes by such things as TV, literature, the Internet, and so on. These things are not bad in and of themselves, but if they are not used responsibly, they can destroy the lives of people and families. Christians should prefer healthy entertainment that is not contrary to biblical values and living a holy life in body, spirit and mind (1 Peter 1:13-17).

c. It is the obligation of every Nazarene believer to testify against everything that offends God or blasphemes against Him. Also, we must raise our voices against social evils, such as injustice and violence. We must reject forms of promotion of sensuality and illicit sex, the use of obscene language, the diffusion of occultism, and love of material things, among others. All these practices undermine the divine standard of holiness of heart and life (1 Thessalonians 4:1-8).

# MARRIAGE AND FAMILY ARE NOT DISPOSABLE

Marriage is not the invention of man or science; it has a divine origin because it was instituted by God in the Garden of Eden, where He created only two sexes, man and woman. Therefore we believe that marriage is sacred and permanent. It also enjoys apostolic approval because in Hebrews 13:4 it says, "Marriage should be honored by all, and the marriage bed kept pure, for God will judge the adulterer and all the sexually immoral."

As Christians renewed in the image of God by His grace, every Nazarene must value the appropriateness of marriage, and its importance to society and the church. It is wise before getting married to pray earnestly for divine direction. When the couple is sure that this union is God's will, then they can ask the Pastor for premarital counseling where they will have an opportunity to reflect on the seriousness of this commitment. The next step is the wedding where the bride and groom request the blessing of God, having understood that marriage is for holy fellowship, parenthood, and mutual love until death separates them.

We must recognize that no marriage is perfect; it begins with a period of adjustments to matrimonial stability, and for this the presence of God in the home is essential to help the couple to be victorious in times of trials or difficult situations. For these moments of crisis, it is advisable to keep in mind the following:

a. When there are serious problems, the spouses should seek in fervent prayer God's direction and guidance.

b. Seek the guidance and counsel of the Pastor or a spiritual guide who should be a mature, confident Christian.

c. Always keep in mind that the Bible teaches that marriage is a lifelong mutual commitment between a man and a woman and reflects the sacrificial love of Christ for the church (Ephesians 5:25-33; Genesis 2:21-24).

d. They always need to remember that the marriage

vow is morally obligatory while both spouses live, and breaking it is disobedience to the divine plan of matrimonial perpetuity (Romans, 7:1-3).

e. Due to human ignorance and weakness, some people break their commitment to marital fidelity. We believe that Christ in His infinite forgiving grace can restore their lives, as long as these people seek with sincere repentance, faith and humility the divine forgiveness of God and forgiveness of their partner (1 John 1:7-9, 2:1-2).

f. Divorce is a clear violation of the teaching of Christ, so each spouse is encouraged to care for their spiritual relationship with Christ to avoid falling into such a situation. However, divorced persons are not beyond the reach of God's forgiving love (Matthew 19:3-10; Malachi 2:13-16).

g. It is the responsibility of the spouses to maintain the marriage harmony, developing family devotions for the purpose of safeguarding their marriages. Marriages well consolidated and united form a Church of the Nazarene which is united and has a good testimony, always honoring the good name of Christ (Psalm 34:11-15).

# THE SPIRIT-FILLED CHRISTIAN OPPOSES MURDER AND VIOLENCE IN ALL OF ITS FORMS

Nazarenes believe that life is sacred from the moment of conception in the womb and that it is a gift of God our Creator. Therefore, every Nazarene must oppose abortion induced by any means when it is used for personal convenience or for population control (Psalm 139:13-16). We must also oppose the passage of laws authorizing abortion, considering that there are very few cases in which doctors diagnose that the mother or unborn child is in danger of not surviving the birth (Exodus 20:13).

Responsible opposition to abortion demands from the church and the believer the following:

a. Educate and guide our parishioners by scheduling special activities for the family in local churches to give workshops, preferably by Christian doctors, on the importance of planned pregnancies and on the sacredness of life as a gift from God (Hosea 4 :6).

b. Develop and initiate social programs in the Churches of the Nazarene for the care of mothers and children who need it (Galatians 6:9-10).

c. Provide our youth with an atmosphere of love, fellowship and counseling about the sacredness of marriage and its importance within the divine plan, so as not to fall into crises of unwanted pregnancies (Exodus 20:14, Hebrews 13:4).

d. Unwanted pregnancies can be avoided if we practice the biblical principles and ethics of Christian life in the New Testament (1 Thessalonians 4:1-8).

## THE SPIRIT-FILLED CHRISTIAN'S VIEW OF SEXUALITY

Nazarenes believe that human sexuality is an expression of the sanctity and beauty that God the Creator provided to his creation. Therefore, believers should be deeply grateful to the Creator for their gender received at birth, with the understanding that only two genders were created by God: man and woman.

Through sex, the covenant between husband and wife is expressed and sealed; keeping in mind that sexuality can and must be sanctified by God. In addition, we need to consider the following aspects about sexuality:

a. Sex is fully realized in marriage as a sign of total love and loyalty (1 Corinthians 7:3-5).

b. Christian spouses should regard sex as a commitment to exclusive surrender and mutual fidelity, just as each individual has promised exclusive fidelity to Christ (Matthew 6:25-34, Luke 12:15).

c. The Christian home should become the first school where we should teach our children the Christian perspective on sex and sexuality (Genesis 1:26-28).

d. Every believer united in marriage is committed to Christ to avoid betrayal of marriage vows and will seek to raise the excellence of married life.

e. Sex does not fulfill its divine purpose when it is

used to satisfy selfish desires, such as prostitution or pornography; Or to satisfy sexual desires in a perverse or unnatural way (such as sex with children, homosexuality, lesbianism, sex with animals, among others).

f.  Every sexual practice outside of marriage is a sinful and a dangerous deviation that damages the sanctity and beauty that God intended to give to sexual relations.

g.  Homosexuality is a perversion of genuine human sexuality, and the remedy prescribed by His Word to end this practice is repentance, seeking the forgiving grace of God (Romans 1:26-27; 1 Corinthians 6:9-11; 1Timothy 1:8-11).

h.  Finally, we recommend that pastors, suitable personnel, doctors or professional leaders of the churches, develop workshops to teach families sexual education, including the true meaning and purpose as well as perversions in the light of the Word of God.

## CONCLUSION:

As we said at the outset, the life of the Spirit-filled believer is full of privileges, blessings and promises, but it also leads us to make a serious commitment to live in holiness following the example of Jesus. Christian ethics teaches us in the Old and New Testaments that a sanctified believer is one who loves God and his neighbor with all his mind and heart (Mark 12:30-31, Deuteronomy 6:5).

We must keep in mind that this holy lifestyle pleases God and produces many healthy benefits for our lives and those of all those around us.

God has enough grace in Christ to empower, strengthen, and affirm each of His children to commit himself to living a holy life that brings honor, glory, and praise to our Creator. To Him be the glory for ever and ever. Amen.

## BIBLIOGRAPHY:

1.  Beacon Bible Commentary, Richard S. Taylor

2.  Christian Perfection, John Wesley

3.  Manual Church of the Nazarene

# SHARING CHRIST WITH MY FAMILY AND FRIENDS

**Juan Manuel Fernández**

## INTRODUCTION

God has made a change in your life. The experience of salvation is the most wonderful that any human can experience. For that reason, God tells us clearly in His Word that He sent His Son to this world "that whoever believes in him shall not perish but have eternal life." (John 3:16). God wants everyone to experience salvation (2 Peter 3:9), and guess what? You are the person God wants and can use to bring the Light to people who now live in darkness.

God calls people to different tasks. Some He calls to be pastors and teachers, others He asks to be musicians or leaders in other areas. But God calls everyone to evangelize! (Matthew 4:19). When Christ ascended to His Father, he left a great mission to all his followers: "Therefore go and make disciples of all nations, baptizing them in the name of the Father and of the Son and of the Holy Spirit," (Matthew 28:19). This is our mission for all who are a part of Christ's church: to tell other people about Him.

This is the most important task in which any Christian can invest his time and the abilities that God has given him. Perhaps your heart has been touched by God, and you feel restlessness in getting ready to share Christ's life with others. The first step is to give your life, through prayer, to the Lord so that you will be filled with the power of the Holy Spirit. (Consecration) You can tell your pastor that you wish to be involved in the evangelism plan of your local church.

This lesson will challenge you as a new believer to begin now to win others to Christ. We want to share with you some simple ways to testify to your friends and family about what Christ has done in your life.

# Why should we tell others about Christ?

We talk about the fact that God calls us to evangelize, in other words, to talk to others about Jesus. But in spite of knowing this, we sometimes have doubts. For example:

**1. "I cannot evangelize because I'm a new Christian and everyone knows that I have been a sinner."**

The Bible tells Paul's story. In the book of Acts, you can read the story of his conversion. Paul was the principal persecutor of the first Christians. After his conversion, Paul immediately surrendered completely to God. He worked side by side with the leaders of the church and started to testify about what God had done in his life (Acts 9:1-20). Don't view the fact that you're a new believer as a disadvantage. On the contrary, this is an advantage. You are experiencing a radical change in your life, and this is the best time to show that change to your family and friends.

(Names and place have been changed.)

Joe is a new believer who lives in the outskirts of Heredia, Costa Rica. He became a Christian in the year 2000, after more than 30 years of living a life of sin. He had done horrible things, even murder. Even his neighbors feared him, because they knew that Joe was a bad man. But one day, God changed his life, and he started to live like a new man. When he spoke to others about Christ, many didn't believe him and they were afraid him. But after a time, people realized that the change in Joe's life was real, and many people accepted Christ through his testimony in the months after his conversion.

God can use your life right now to reach others for his Kingdom. Don't waste this opportunity!

**2. "I want to tell others what God has done in my life, but I'm not good at speaking and I am also very young."**

In the Bible, we can see examples of people who had impediments to talk well, or simply were not good speakers, or were very shy about sharing the message of God with others.

Moses, one of the greatest leaders of the Old Testament,

had an impediment of this type. For that reason, God sent Aaron to help him communicate. If you have an impediment of this type, God can still use you. How? Go with a Christian friend when you visit your non-Christian friends and family. You will be surprised at what God can do.

We also can see the example of Jeremiah, a prophet who was afraid of testifying because he was so young. God touched his lips and all his doubts were taken away, and he became one of the greatest prophets of the Old Testament. Our God is all-powerful, and is owner of all things. His Word says that if we pray with faith, He will answer our prayers. Ask God to help you be a blessing to others in communicating his message, in spite of whatever impediments you might have.

**3. "I want to talk to my family about Christ, but they are so far away from Him that they are never going to change."**

This is one of the biggest lies that Satan uses to impede God's children from sharing His divine message with others. The Devil is our enemy and he doesn't want us to take the message of salvation to other people. For that reason, he will try to plant doubts in our mind to avoid sharing. The Bible assures us that anyone who prays with faith and believes in Christ Jesus, he or she will be saved and their sins will be forgiven. Just as God forgave your sins, He also wants to forgive your family and friends.

# What is the best way to talk to others about Christ?

Now that you are a member of God's Family, it's time to start talking to others about Christ. There are two key factors that you must include when you talk about Christ: your testimony and your communication.

### 1. Your testimony

One of the most effective ways to share the gospel is when someone becomes a believer and people can see in his or her life an example of what Christ can do in the believer's life. In this way, we can testify to friends and family. A good testimony is based on a life that reflects the fullness of the

Holy Spirit. You can reach that friend or co-worker, even if you don't have the confidence to talk to them about Christ, through your testimony. That person will notice the change and will ask you, What has happened to you? When you have reached this point, the person will be receptive to the gospel message.

## 2. Your Communication

Although it is important to testify about Christ through our example, our oral communication is no less important in reaching that other person. The Bible assures us in Isaiah 55:11, "so is my word that goes out from my mouth: It will not return to me empty, but will accomplish what I desire and achieve the purpose for which I sent it." Therefore, the Word of God affirms that a biblical verse is more powerful than all words that we can say, no matter how good of a speaker we are. Therefore it is key that when you talk with someone about Christ, you frequently refer to the Bible. There are five biblical truths to mention when we talk to others about Christ:

**First Truth:** God loves you and he wants you to be saved. God has loved us with an everlasting love (Jeremiah 31:3) and for that reason, He sent his son to die for us (John 3:16). He has a great plan for all who accept him as his or her Savior (John 10:10).

**Second Truth:** Sin separates us from God. Why doesn't everyone accept Christ as their Savior? It's because of sin. The Bible says that we all are sinful (Romans 3:23), and for that reason, we are separated from God. Because of sin, man forfeits his relationship with God and is condemned to death (Romans 5:12). Man was created by God to be good and to have companionship with Him, but man sinned, and caused his separation from God (Geneses 3), bringing to himself painful consequences. Because of sin, today the world is full of wickedness, thefts, murders, etc.

**Third Truth:** Christ died to cleanse us from our sins. God, in his infinite mercy, sent his Son Jesus Christ to die for man's sins. The Word of God tells us, "But God demonstrates his own love for us in this: While we were still sinners, Christ died for us" (Romans 5:8). Jesus died in our place. He took our place as sinners who were destined to eternal death, and He gives us the opportunity to have eternal life.

**Fourth Truth:** Christ is the only way to salvation. Thanks to Christ's sacrifice, we only need to pray a prayer of faith to be forgiven of our sins and have eternal life. Jesus Christ made this possible, and for that reason, He is the Savior and the only way for the relationship between God and us to be restored. Christ says, "Nobody comes to the Father except through me" (John 14:6).

**Fifth Truth:** We can accept the gift of salvation by having faith. The prayer of repentance should be made with faith. If we believe that Christ is the Savior, and that He cleans us of all sin, we will receive eternal life because of our faith. Faith is believing in God and putting all of our trust in Christ. Salvation cannot be earned by our achievements or by doing good things (Ephesians 2:8, 9). God gives eternal life to everyone who invites Christ into his or her heart and follows him by becoming His disciple.

If you have explained these five steps to someone, and they have understood them, then you can ask them this question, "Would you like to receive Christ into your life?" If that person says "no," or says that he or she is not yet ready to do so, thank them and continue praying for them. If that person says yes, ask them to repeat the following brief prayer which summarizes the five points that you mentioned. The prayer should be said slowly, allowing the other person to repeat the words after you. This is an example:

*"Jesus Christ, I understand that you love me and that you died on the cross to cleanse me from my sins. I am a sinner, and there is nothing that I can do on my own to be clean of my sins. I know that you take away the guilt of my sins. Jesus, you are my Savior and the only way to the Father. I ask you to forgive me of my sins and give me a new life and relationship with you. Thank you for the work that you will do in my life, starting today. Amen"*

Congratulations! If you have helped another person say this prayer, God has used you to bring salvation to him or her. Now there is a celebration in heaven! (Luke 15:7).

You can give assurance to the new believer by reading to

them what Christ said in John 6:47, "Very truly I tell you, the one who believes has eternal life."

Then, it is important for you to encourage him to join a class or discipleship group, or you can disciple him or her yourself using the lessons "New Life in Christ" that you can get from your pastor or online. Later on you will find more recommendations to make sure that this baby in Christ grows spiritually.

# How do I choose the best time to talk to someone about Christ?

There are many situations that can influence how someone will respond when the salvation message is presented to him or her.

### 1. Prayer

Prayer is the key to evangelism. If you want to talk about Christ to somebody like a relative, a friend, or an unknown person, it is vital that you have a time of prayer before talking with them, and that you ask God to prepare their hearts for His message. If you pray for a few months before talking to someone about Christ, I assure you that you will get better results than if you simply improvise (Matthew 6:6). This doesn't mean that if you don't pray previously for somebody, this person won't become a Christian. Don't forget to be spontaneous and seize the moments that God gives you to evangelize. Try to pray for the people that God has placed in your life for you to reach for His Kingdom. If you work where you are in contact with people every day, then you should ask God to prepare you and the people that you see each day, so that He will touch/prepare their hearts. Prayer is the most powerful tool we can use to bring people to Jesus.

### 2. Acts of Compassion

Acts of compassion are great ways for the Christian to show Christ's love in a concrete and interesting way. If you have prayed for a neighbor, show him God's love before presenting the gospel to him: take him lunch, invite him to have dinner with you, help him with his garden or wash his car, etc. Find his specific needs, and then whenever it is possible, meet those needs without wanting anything in return.

When people receive help, they are receiving the touch of God's love, and they will be more receptive to hear about Jesus.

### 3. Moments of good receptivity

All people go through stages of their life in which they are more receptive to the message of the gospel. If you pray, do acts of compassion, and also learn how to recognize these moments of good receptivity, you will multiply the opportunities for that person to accept Christ as his or her Lord and Savior.

The moments of greatest receptivity to the gospel are usually times of personal or family change (marriage, the birth of a child, a new job, moving, etc.); in times of crisis or loss (death, illness or accident, divorce or marriage tensions, economic setback, etc.); or times of social tension (recession, natural catastrophes, war, crime, violence, etc.).

### 4. Identification with the receiver

The best results in personal evangelism are when people witness to those with whom they have much in common. For that reason, you are the best evangelist in the world to your friends and family, and those with whom you share time every day. You know about their needs, their hopes, and their sorrows, and you have Christ - the message of hope that they need!

## How can I talk about Christ with someone who doesn't want to know anything about Him?

It is difficult to present Christ to people who have hardened their hearts. In today's world, where so much of Christ is spoken of negatively through the media, there are many people who have closed their hearts in such a way that it seems virtually impossible to reach them.

The best thing that one can do for those people is to pray, asking God to touch their hearts, and to help you discern the best moment to talk to them about Christ. The way you share/present the gospel should vary depending on the person. There are some cases in which insisting on talking about Christ is the best thing, while in other cases, pushing will only make things worse. Ask God for wisdom, as Solomon did, and He will guide you to make the correct decision. Also, there are people in your church with more experience in evangelism who can offer valuable advice.

## What other methods can I use to tell someone about Christ?

The Lord has given us many methods to reach people for His Kingdom. One of the most effective methods is the "Jesus" film.

The "Jesus" film has been shown since 1979, and it is estimated that already more than four and half billion people have seen the film, and more than a hundred million people have accepted Christ because of the film. More than thirty three million video cassettes and DVDs of the "Jesus" film exist in almost eight hundred languages.

All you must do is pray for the person and then invite him/her to watch the movie or lend him the video. At the end, the movie includes an invitation to accept Christ. If you need a copy of the movie, you may be able to get it from your pastor.

Another resource for evangelism is the evangelism cube. This cube has seven panels, and each panel has a picture that presents part of the salvation message. This method has also produced very good results. In August of 2002, in the City of Guatemala, over 350 people received Jesus Christ in one week. This cube is not magic, but is a great resource for people to use to communicate the gospel clearly and in an interesting way. A lot of people who have never shared the gospel before can share it using the EvangeCube. The EvangeCube is available in a number of places. Ask your pastor to give you more information.

These are only examples of some tools that you can use to reach others for Christ. The important thing is that you use all your creativity to find the best way to communicate the gospel to people.

# My friend accepted Christ. Now what?

Your friend or relative has accepted Christ, and the most wonderful experience in his life has just begun. Now he or she is a member of God's family. Now they are a new disciple of Christ, and who better than you to disciple them?

The best thing that you can do to help him grow in his new life is to give him the first lesson of discipleship, "New Life in Christ", within the first 48 hours after his/her prayer of faith. It is important to meet with him at least one hour each week in the following days.

It is best if you can meet with them in their house, because there will be opportunities for their family to also listen to the message of the gospel, and they too may become interested in the bible study. This is also the best method to begin new ministries in the houses of new believers.

With the Level B lessons of discipleship, the new believers can be prepared for baptism in a few weeks and continue on to be filled with the Holy Spirit, and to become members of the church.

The best thing that you can do for the new believer is to assimilate them into God's Family. It is part of your responsibility to invite them to the worship services of your church and to introduce them to the pastor and other believers. You have the blessed responsibility to help take care of them and to feed them the Word as they mature in their faith.

# Notes:

# GOD, THE OWNER OF ALL THINGS

**Mónica Mastronardi de Fernández, Rubén E. Fernández**

## WHO IS THE OWNER?

An old man once complained that his grandson had borrowed his guitar the year before and had never returned it. The young man was indignant that his grandfather wanted him to return it because he had arthritis and could not play the guitar. He said angrily, "You no longer need it." Some people believe that having something and using it for a while makes them the owners. If you are one of those people, you need to understand the difference between having possession of something and owning it.

For some people, to own something means to have rights over it; that is why the old man in our story asked his grandson to return something he considered his own. In our world, the legal "owner" can use, abuse and sell what belongs to him. But for the people who make up the church of Christ, the idea of ownership is different. In Acts 4:32, it says of the early Christians, "No one claimed that any of their possessions was their own."

So, are we or are we not owners of the things we have and that we consider ours? If we are not the owners, then who is? There are three possible answers that we can consider.

The idea of the individual as owner has had many advocates especially in the last century. This idea has justified the rights of people to live in selfishness without feeling guilty. Legislation in many countries is based on this way of thinking and therefore justifies the materialistic attitude of people or families who have enough to help others and do not want to do so. But Jesus did not share this view. He recounted a story of a rich man named Dives who refused to give help to Lazarus a beggar, and Jesus condemned this attitude (Luke 16:19-31).

Another idea, contrary to the previous one, is to consider the community or group of people as the owners. Some find a biblical basis in Acts 2:44-45 where it says that, "All the believers were together and had everything in common. They sold property and possessions to give to anyone who had need." Also in Acts 4:32 it says that "they shared everything they had." But there are no further references in the New Testament that this was a widespread practice in all the churches, but rather in some groups of disciples who were very excited and hoped that Jesus would return from heaven very soon.

If the community is not the true owner, then who is? 1 Timothy 6:7 says, "For we brought nothing into the world, and we can take nothing out of it." In the Bible, the one who has the rights as the owner is the one who has something without having received it from anyone. Under these parameters, neither individuals nor the community qualify as owners, since they have received everything they have. The Bible points out that God is the only one who owns the universe, so the apostle Paul asks, "What do you have that you did not receive? And if you did receive it, why do you boast as though you did not?" (1 Corinthians 4:7).

What legitimate rights does God have to declare Himself the Master of all things?

## GOD IS THE CREATOR OF EVERYTHING THAT EXISTS

The biblical account starts with these words: "In the beginning, God created the heavens and the earth" (Genesis 1:1).

This account of Genesis 1 explains how God formed the whole universe by a free act of His sovereign will. This work was done step by step and in an orderly way. It began by bringing into existence the four basic elements: earth, water, air, and fire, and with this raw material He gave shape to all living organisms.

This truth revealed in the Scriptures was accepted without problems until the scientists Darwin, Huxley, Spencer among others, questioned it. They tried to prove that God had nothing to do with the appearance on the planet of all life forms, but that they evolved from each other giving rise to all the species that have existed and exist today.

However, serious and world-renowned scientists such as Sir Cecil Wakeley, Sir Ambrose Fleming and Louis Agassiz, claim that this theory of evolution is indeed a "new religion", since its theories have not been scientifically proven and can therefore only be believed by faith.

This false religion has left God out of the universe and has given rise to every false and anti-Christian "ism" that has arisen in the last hundred years. Hitler, for example, took his ideas for the superior race from the evolutionist Nietzsche, justifying the slaughter of millions of people. Mussolini, citing Darwin in his speeches, affirmed that the idea of peace was not conceivable because of the concept of the survival of the fittest or for the perfection of the human race, thus justifying war. Karl Marx based his communist theories on Darwin's postulates, thus justifying his atheistic doctrines[1] and the persecution and torture of Christians.

In spite of all the efforts of these scientists to erase the idea of a God as the Creator from the human mind, instead of corroborating the assumptions of evolutionists, contemporary science is coming up with new evidence of the truth of the Biblical story of creation. Today thanks to technological advances, science has verified many of the statements of the story of Genesis 1 and 2.

Let's look at some examples. Genesis 1:1 says that the whole universe originated in a great moment or in a first second of life. This has been corroborated by observing the behavior of galaxies that continue to expand at increasingly accelerating speeds. These findings by researchers Jun and Gustav Tamman may overturn the Bing Bang theory that the universe had originated in an explosion of energy that expanded the matter of the planets, which existed but was condensed, and that this expansion would not continue forever but would retract itself by gravitational forces and thus the universe for all eternity would continue to recreate itself.[2]

Some examples of other facts of the divine creation verified today by science are:

- Water appeared on our planet in liquid form before it was formed as stated in Genesis 1:6.[3]

- Plant life existed before animal life (Genesis 1:11, 20).

- The moon was formed after the earth (Gen 1:14-15).[4]

- The first living creatures arose in water (Gen 1:20), birds existed before mammals (Gen 1:20 and 25), and humans were the last to appear on the face of the earth (Gen 1:26).

- Human beings are unique among living creatures because of their well-defined characteristics that give them superiority over other forms of life (Genesis 1:26-27).

- The human brain has been designed with the ability to relate to God. Man is a spiritual creature who has the need to communicate with the Creator God and Governor of the universe (Gen.1:27).

The author of Hebrews wrote, "By faith we understand that the universe was formed at God's command, so that what is seen was not made out of what was visible" (Hebrews 11:3) ).

In the past it was hard to believe that material arose from immaterial forces. But today there is no doubt that matter can be produced by energy. This is just what the biblical account says. God is the source of all that exists, the only source of life that can give rise to other lives.

In other words, we can affirm that everything material has a spiritual origin, because everything comes from God and God is Spirit (John 4:24).

## GOD SUSTAINS HIS CREATION

Colossians 1:17 affirms that, "He is before all things, and in him all things hold together." Our lives and that of all creation depend on God. Just as a car cannot run without gas, the universe would cease to exist without the power of God to sustain it.

God has not departed from His Creation by leaving it to its fate. On the contrary, again and again the Lord declares in his Word that He is in control of His Creation and that life would not continue without His loving care. The prophet Jeremiah said, "He made the earth by his power; he founded the world by his wisdom and stretched out the heavens by his understanding. When he thunders, the waters in the heavens roar; he makes clouds rise from the ends of the earth. He sends lightning with the rain and brings out the wind from his storehouses" (Jeremiah 51:15-16).

Later the author of Hebrews states that it is the Son of God, Jesus Christ who sustains the whole universe by the life-giving power of his word: "...but in these last days he has spoken to us by his Son, whom he appointed heir of all things, and through whom also he made the universe. The Son is the radiance of God's glory and the exact representation of his being, sustaining all things by his powerful word" (Hebrews 1:2-3).

Also in this same chapter, the author of the letter to the Hebrews emphasizes that the ultimate destiny of our world and the universe is in the hands of Jesus Christ and not of human beings (Hebrews 1:10-12).

## GOD'S PURPOSE FOR HIS CREATION

God created the universe and everything within it with the potential to grow and develop. "Be fruitful and increase in number; fill the earth and subdue it" (Genesis 1:28). God's purpose for every living being is to develop to their fullest potential.

It is possible to observe how nature obeys the Creator by growing and expanding, giving continual testimony to humankind of the infinite wisdom of the Lord (Proverbs 3:19-20). God is the source of wisdom for our life and wants us to live close to Him in order not to miss the way (Proverbs 8).

Human beings like all other creatures are destined to grow in all dimensions: physical, mental, emotional, social and spiritual.

## GOD'S PURPOSE FOR MEN AND WOMEN

Throughout history human beings have wondered what the purpose or reason of their existence is? Where do we come from? Where are we going? Are our lives something destined to be lost in the abyss of time? Is the body something only to be destined to mix with the dust of the earth? Is it worth living? What is the meaning of life, work, study, and love?

All of these are legitimate questions but fall into the void when people try to answer them by ignoring the Author of life. The universe was not created by chance, but because God had a holy plan or purpose for it. When we try to live our lives ignoring the purpose of God by going our own ways, we live in sin.

We are the supreme reason why God created the world (Romans 8:18-23). We are not the product of a cellular mutation that evolved by accident, but are the result of a perfectly designed divine plan.

We are different from other created beings. We are not "evolved animals" as Darwin's followers claim. Despite having many things in common with other living beings, we were designed by God for a special purpose, and have been endowed with unique characteristics that distinguish us from other living beings (1 Cor. 15:39). These particular and unique characteristics are due to our being made in the image of God.

"Then God said, 'Let us make mankind in our image, in our likeness, so that they may rule over the fish in the sea and the birds in the sky, over the livestock and all the wild animals, and over all the creatures that move along the ground.' So God created mankind in his own image, in the image of God he created them" (Genesis 1:26-27).

This image of God, given to man and woman, makes them superior to the rest of the creatures; it is what allows them to enjoy fellowship with God and allows them to have freedom to decide their own destiny.

We are capable of experiencing happiness and satisfaction. God created man and woman to be happy. The Creator put our first parents in a paradise garden where all beings lived in harmony. The couple had a perfect relationship with God, with the rest of creation and with each other.

But this happiness for which we were created has nothing to do with the modern concept of the pursuit of pleasure to gratify the senses. We were created to achieve happiness through self-realization; the satisfaction of knowing that with our lives we are contributing to an important project that benefits others and not only ourselves.

We were not created to be selfish, or for the enjoyment of the senses, or to live far from God's companionship. We have been endowed by God to actively participate in the task of sustaining life. This is why the functions of Adam and Eve are described as working the garden and taking care of it (Gen 2:15).

We have been given superior intelligence, capable of learning, of creating and of reasoning. Even though of all living beings we are the most defenseless at birth, we are the only ones with more developed intelligence. This allows us, among other things, to participate in making decisions as to our own development and destiny, unlike animals.

We have been endowed with consciousness, a triple consciousness that distinguishes us from the animal kingdom, allowing us to relate in three dimensions:

a) **With the surrounding world**, which we know, experience and understand through our senses (taste, sight, smell, hearing, touch). We are sensitive and have the ability to respond to the stimuli of the environment we experience with our physical bodies.

b) **Our inner being**, or soul, ego or self, which makes us unique personalities with wills and freedom to choose.

c) **We have the ability to know God and to relate to Him through His Spirit**, who also gives us a higher consciousness that allows us to differentiate what is good from what is bad. God endowed us with moral personality, or with freedom or the free will to choose between good and evil. So in this sense, we are equal before God, since He wanted from the beginning to form a people (church) that will serve and adore Him voluntarily. God does not want slaves, or robots in His service, but children who truly love him above all things.

d) **We were created to be "holy".** While this term does not appear in the account of Genesis 1-3, it is clear that God's purpose for them was to live apart from all evil. Evil is everything that is opposed to the will of God. While Adam and Eve were doing the will of God, their happiness and that of the rest of the creatures that depended on them was guaranteed. God created them holy in spirit, soul and body, as they had not yet been defiled by evil.

God gave us these qualities so that we can successfully fulfill the vocation for which we were created: to be His "stewards". A steward is a person who manages the possessions of the owner. God expects all his children to serve Him on earth as His responsible stewards (Gen 1:26-28).

## THE RIGHTS OF THE
## OWNER ARE USURPED

For a long time the rights of the Creator to be the ruler of His creation have been challenged. In the Bible, Lucifer, one of God's most beautiful angels, wanted to usurp God's place as owner and became His enemy (John 12:31, 14:30, 16:11). Since then, Satan has been dedicated to tempting and seducing human beings to submit to his authority and reject the will of God for their lives.

The fate of all creation is linked to the permanence of the human race in the divine plan. When Adam and Eve deliberately crossed the boundaries that God had pointed out to them (Genesis 2:16; 3:1-24), they brought for themselves and for all creation and for their descendants, pain and suffering. In the Bible, disobedience to a known law of God is called "sin." As sin entered the human race, a barrier of separation between man and God arose.

Adam and Eve's act of disobedience was a decision that affected them and all their descendants to this day. They turned their backs on God, disobeyed His will, and "tasted" sinning, instead of rejecting it.

The tree in the middle of the garden was not put there by God to tempt them, but to remind them that evil exists. The possibility of sin was always there; the possibility of turning their back on God was always there.

If they resisted the temptation that Satan presented to them, their will would have been strengthened greatly. But in choosing the path of disobedience, sin made its entrance. Consequently, the perfect balance and harmony that characterized their way of life were damaged. Adam and Eve lost their holiness and their perfect relationship with God, with creation.

God's plan was not for mankind to know evil, but to be able to perceive it compared to His holiness. But when they listened to the words of the serpent (Satan), Adam and Eve choose to know evil and experienced a broken relationship with God.

God's plan was altered when human beings came to know and experience what evil was and sinned. Now we can only imagine what it would have been like to live in the good and perfect happiness of the holy life and in harmony with the purposes of God. For people who have not yet repented of their sins, it is difficult to grasp God's purpose for His creation, but it is even more difficult to accept and willingly participate in this plan.

Sin has a destructive power. It's like rust that corrodes even hard metal. We humans cannot rid ourselves of sin and its consequences, which could have ultimately destroy the whole of God's Creation. To prevent such a tragedy, God sent us the perfect remedy in His Son, Jesus Christ.

## GOD RESCUES HIS CREATION THROUGH JESUS CHRIST

In some of our countries, there has grown in recent years the criminal modality of kidnapping to request sums of money. These people do not steal goods but steal people and hold them captive until the ransom price has been delivered. People who are taken from their families suffer without knowing if they will ever meet again with their loved ones. These sad stories that move us often help us understand what God as the Creator Father feels for all who have been alienated from His side and remain prisoners of sin.

The people who have been abducted cannot pay the ransom for themselves. They need some family member who wants to "redeem" them, someone who loves them enough to pay the price that the kidnappers have asked for to save their lives. This is what God did in sending His only Son, "who gave himself for us to redeem us from all wickedness and to purify for himself a people that are his very own, eager to do what is good" (Titus 2:14).

This means that God bought us and the price He paid was the life of his Son (1 Corinthians 6:20). The work that God the Father entrusted to His Son was to end the curse that sin brought to the entire human race as well as to the rest of Creation. Now we are His because we are His creation, but doubly His because He has bought us back.

# GOD RESTORES HIS CREATION THROUGH THE HOLY SPIRIT

In addition to being our Creator who rescues us from the chains of sin, God wants to restore us so that we can live according to the plan He has for our lives (1 Cor. 6:11). Jesus Christ has provided us with an example of a clean life free of sin (Romans 8:29).

Jesus Christ became man to reconquer all that the first Adam had lost. The Bible tells us that Jesus Christ is the second Adam who triumphed in everything that the first Adam failed (1 Cor. 15:45).

God wants us to live this kind of life by putting within us His Holy Spirit who helps us become more and more like Jesus, transforming us more into His image of holiness; the 'glory' that the Father wants all his children to reflect (2 Cor. 3:18).

Through Jesus Christ, God showed that He still trusts us and wants to count on us to be His holy instruments to look after the earth and allow it to express fully the glory of the Creator. But to become responsible stewards, Christians need to meet certain requirements which are listed below.

# CHARACTERISTICS OF GOOD ADMINISTRATORS

**The first characteristic of good stewards is that they must "dedicate" their lives and all that they have to God and His work.** On one occasion when they asked Jesus if it was right to pay taxes, He replied, " ...give back to Caesar what is Caesar's, and to God what is God's" (Matthew 22:21). If God tells you today, "Give me everything you have", what is God asking you to give?

Recognizing that God is the owner of all things leads us to see things and our own lives with different eyes. They are no longer "our things" but everything belongs to God. This is the difference between being a steward or the owner. Stewards are those people in whom the owner entrusts his valuable possessions so that they can administer them with wisdom. Christians are stewards and should dedicate themselves wholly to live for and to serve God. The word "dedicate" means to put aside something for a special use. This does not imply that someone has the right to demand that you sell your home or your car and deliver the money to the church. But God wants you to recognize in your heart that all that has been given to you is not yours in reality, but it is God who has given you the responsibility to care for those things. God as the owner also has the right to ask for what he has given us when he needs it, including our life.

**The second quality of good stewards is that they are grateful.** When someone gives us a gift that is valuable to us, we feel grateful. Likewise in recognizing that it is God who has given us "all things," gratitude should flows spontaneously from our hearts (Romans 8:32).

When people do not thank God for everything they have received from His hand, they are evil (Romans 1:21). Gratitude is a vital part of the Christian life. It is one of the reasons that leads us to worship God and serve Him for His generosity towards us and our family.

We should not be grateful only for material things. We live in a society in love with things. But God gives us everything and much more than material goods such as; life, husband, wife, friends, brothers and sisters in the faith, parents, the ability to learn, sight, touch and smell. He gives us an abundance of fruit in nature, the company of animals, and thousands of more things which are priceless.

**The third quality of good stewards is obedience.** Because he is our owner, God exercises dominion over us. He is the sovereign Lord of our life. He is our King.

The Bible says that we cannot call Jesus Lord if we are not willing to obey Him (Luke 6:46). Nothing further damages the testimony of God's people than believers who worship God in the church and then live in continual disobedience to God outside of church.

God asks us to be faithful, that is, to respond to the confidence he has placed in us (1 Cor. 4:1-2). God wants us to use what we have, material possessions, personal abilities, our time or anything else, to serve Him and not just to satisfy our own needs.

For example, if God has given us abilities for teaching, He not only wants us to use this to earn our livelihood, but to invest this gift in His work.

It is very important also that stewards live in a way that honors God. Otherwise people will get the wrong idea. If a leader treats people badly in the church, folks may come to think that God is like that. But if people observe the good things that God's children do, then they will praise their Father in heaven (Matthew 5:16). Integrity and faithfulness are qualities required of good stewards.

**A fourth quality of good stewards mentioned in the Bible is wisdom.** Wisdom is practical intelligence enabling us to make the best decisions. A wise steward will use resources wisely, avoid waste, and distribute goods to meet needs, maintain an orderly record of business, and take advantage of opportunities presented. This is how stewards increase the owners' profits. The Bible contains many lessons of wisdom for us as stewards and instructs us in the Christian way of investing our lives as well as the resources entrusted to us.

# KEYS TO BECOMING GOOD INVESTORS

Investment means buying something for the purpose of making a profit. Buying a bag of rice to eat with your family is an expense. But if you buy a bag of rice to prepare food and then sell it, you are making an investment. This is also true when we invest our time, skills or belongings for God, because He has promised that He will continually give us much more than we give so that we can continue to invest. This is what God promises in His Word, "Whoever sows sparingly will also reap sparingly, and whoever sows generously will also reap generously. Each of you should give what you have decided in your heart to give, not reluctantly or under compulsion, for God loves a cheerful giver. And God is able to bless you abundantly, so that in all things at all times, having all that you need, you will abound in every good work" (2 Cor. 9:6-8).

God has revealed to us in His Word the keys to success about how we invest what he has given us:

### Key 1: Give generous offerings for the support and extension of the church.

From the earliest times, believers have practiced the custom of giving a tenth of their income to God. This is called "tithe" (Leviticus 27:30-32). Thanks to Christians who have been faithful in giving their tithes throughout history, the church has been sustained and the gospel continues to spread throughout the world.

Giving our tithes is a privilege of all God's children. But we can do more than that. True Christians are characterized by grateful hearts and by giving generous offerings for God's work. Sometimes we think that those who have the most are those who must sustain the work of the church. But in fact history tells us that it is the believers who have given offerings sacrificially who have made possible the miracle of the spreading the gospel to all the continents. Giving an offering sacrificially means to deprive oneself of something and give what it was worth as an offering to God. It is giving up our rights of enjoying something that "We have earned" with our effort, to meet the needs of others.

### Key 2: Giving to other people in need.

Jesus said, "Freely you have received; freely give" (Matthew 10:8). This means that just as God gives us all that we have with generosity, so we must give ourselves to others in need. In the parable of the talents of Matthew 25:15, Jesus taught that we can all give something. In doing good to others we must include those of our own family, brothers and sisters in the faith, and all those who have needs (poor, sick, etc.).

### Key 3: Meet our own needs.

God also wants us to take care of ourselves and our family. He cares about our well-being. Good investors save up for times of scarcity and need.

# References

1. Atheist: a person who denies the existence of God

2. "Finding a birthplace of stars" published in La Nación newspaper, San José, Costa Rica, Friday, April 6, 2001, page 22A, based on studies by researchers at the National Radio Astronomy Observatory and the Anglo Australian Observatory in Sydney. The conclusions of Jun and Tammann on the studies carried out during 15 years in the telescope of 200 inches of the observatory of Monte Palomar published in the magazine Time 30 of December of 1974 p. 48 quoted by D. James Kennedy in "Why I Believe." Editorial Life 1982: Miami, page 52.

3. "Revealed antiquity of water " in newspaper La Nación, San José, Costa Rica, Sunday, January 21, 2001. Page 34A, based on studies published by the Institute of Astrobiology of the US Space Agency (NASA).

4. Article: "How was the moon born?" In La Nación newspaper, San José, Costa Rica, Thursday, August 16, 2001, based on work by American scientists published in the journal Nature.

# Bibliography

Anderson, Neil y Saucy, Robert. The Common Made Holy. Unilit, Miami, 1997.

Flores, José. The Text of the New Testament.

Franco, Sergio. Approach to the Study of the Bible,

Purkiser, W. T. A View of Biblical Doctrine,

Robertson A. T., Verbal Images of the N.T. Barcelona, 1988.

Sauer, Erich, The Dawn of World Redemption.

# YOU WILL RECEIVE POWER

Stephen Manley

## The Question of the Moment

The disciples came to Jesus with this question: "Lord, are you at this time going to restore the kingdom to Israel?" (Acts 1:6b). They insisted on obtaining an answer. The first part of the verse is: "So when they met together, they asked him," (Acts 1:6a). The verb "asked" is in the imperfect tense, which implies that the disciples asked him this question repeatedly, and they urged Jesus to give them a response.

"He said to them: 'It is not for you to know the times or dates the Father has set by his own authority.'"(Acts 1:7). In a literal sense, Jesus was telling them "Don't be concerned with what doesn't matter." The question that they asked was focused on a mistaken subject. The disciples are worried about when the event would occur and that was not to be their concern.

When reflecting about my prayer life, I observe that same emphasis in my prayers. I'm maybe not as specific as the disciples, but I have the same attitude in the tone and desire of my prayers. That same tone is in all of my relationship with Jesus: When will he heal my body? When will he solve my financial problems? When will he save my dear friends? When will he give me a new job? When will he return for the second time?

### An Inappropriate Question

The disciples question is strong: "Lord, will you restore the Kingdom to Israel at this time?" Their question is not only "when?" but rather it demands the answer be now. This is the constant emphasis in the life of the disciples. They discussed who would be first in the Kingdom of God. They wanted Jesus to decide immediately (Mathew 18:1; 20:21). On the Mount of Transfiguration, Peter wanted to build three shelters and to establish immediately what he believed was to be the Kingdom of God (Mathew 17:4). And here they come again with "now" as the correct time.

This is the characteristic of the current generation. We have microwaves to prepare food instantly, fast food restaurants, and chapels for instant marriages. We have instantaneous experiences by means of television, we buy lottery tickets to become rich overnight, and we even have express service to have the oil changed in our cars.

In this context, we want the same thing in our spiritual experience with Christ. We don't want the praise and worship service to extend for more than one hour. He (the pastor) should keep to the necessary minimum! We don't want a long and deep investigation of God´s word, we say please just tell us a story. Our devotional books are made to see the Bible quickly, so it doesn't take a lot of time. We want to be as spiritual as Jesus, but very quickly. I fear that it is a diabolical model.

## The Time of God

The Temptation of Jesus in Mathew 4:1-11 began this way: "After fasting forty days and forty nights, he was hungry" (Mathews 4:2). This period of time is the model of God. He was not in a hurry. It was not two or three hours of prayer in the church. Jesus was not thinking of "now", but rather was looking for communion with the Father. The devil's model is evident in Jesus' temptation. Each temptation was focused on the immediate thing. If Jesus was hungry, he simply should "tell the stones to become bread" (Mathew 4:3b). Don't wait, get it now.

The second temptation was on the highest point of the temple. The devil suggested that Jesus jump and let the angels save him. This would prove that He was the Son of God. He would not have to spend three years in ministry and go to the cross. A simple jump from the highest point would be enough. Why wait?

The third temptation was a glance at all the kingdoms of the earth. Satan offered all the kingdoms to Jesus in exchange for a simple moment of worship to him. The purpose of Jesus coming to earth, according to Satan, had been reached in that moment, instead of on the cross. This is the way the devil thinks. Jesus didn't spare words to tell his disciples that their focus was mistaken. "The times or dates" were none of their concern. The two words of "times" and "dates" don't refer to the same thing, but together they cover the entirety of what is called prophecy.

The Greek word that translates as "times" means periods of the same duration. This makes reference to the prophetic times and the intervals between them. The Greek word that translates as "dates" means the specific time for the execution of a prophetic event. It is not of our concern and we should not focus ourselves in particular on a moment or time or even on a general period of time.

Jesus was specific in telling the disciples that this should not be their focus. He used the words "by his own authority" This word means the power to give orders or make decisions. In Greek, the expression "authority" is a word that implies something much stronger than power. It is an adjective that means "private" or "personal." This is something that really belongs only to God. Such information is totally beyond the jurisdiction of the disciples and it won't be discovered by anybody, no matter how diligently they investigate.

## What Concerns the Disciples

Jesus established the exclusive responsibility of God. What the disciples wanted to know was none of their concern. He began the following phrase with the conjunction "but" (Acts 1:8). He wanted to contrast what didn't concern them with something that really affected them. He completed a picture and then presented a contrasting picture. On the one side was what the disciples could not know. "But" marks another expression that he revealed what they could know. He said it clearly: "But you will receive power when the Holy Spirit comes on you; and you will be my witnesses in Jerusalem, and in all Judea and Samaria, and to the ends of the earth." (Acts 1:8).

I must admit that I have fought with this text. It is easy to see it in a superficial way and to use it as an introduction for a class in personal evangelism. But this verse, seen in its context, takes us to a depth that we should not miss. I'm not sure of being able to communicate it or even to understand it. Maybe I should dwell in this verse for a few years.

## You Will Be My Witnesses

It is very important that we see this verse as a whole. The issue should not be treated as only one part of Christianity that is emphasized from time to time. The concept that this verse presents is the whole of Christianity. This is a summary of the heartbeat of God. It is the soul of the gospel. Everything in this verse points to the concept of "you will be my witness." The verse opens up with a declaration of the power necessary to make Christianity a reality. Luke closes the verse telling where this must be fulfilled. So, everything in this verse brings us back to the central point of "you will be my witnesses."

We should not deceive ourselves thinking that we must only be witnesses during special times of the Christian calendar. Nor to think that to be witnesses is a spiritual discipline or basic doctrine to which we must give special attention, like tithing, reading the Bible, praying, and among these include witnessing. This can be true if you are presenting a diluted version of testifying, of being witness, but that it is not the point that Jesus presents in this verse.

Luke, in the Book of Acts, used the term "witness" in a special way. This gives a unique importance to the term. A witness is someone who was with Jesus when certain events occurred. A witness can tell what he knows because he was there. The gospel is a revelation of our history, and we know about definite facts. However, the witness endorses the true facts within himself. Anyone can memorize academic data. Anyone can memorize a plan of personal evangelism and recite Bible verses by heart, but this is not what Luke wanted to say.

Luke described events that are to become the believer's own experience. The truth is now part of the witness. There are events of the life of Jesus that anyone can know. However, when those events are made reality, truth in our life, then Jesus is reality in our life because He is the Truth. Luke presents to us the great events of the gospel, but when, by faith, we make those events ours, Jesus embraces us. Jesus becomes the point of focus of all our life. In Luke's concept, it is impossible to experience these events without uniting with the Person of Christ. We are to be focused on Him, to be his witnesses.

## You Will Receive Power

This is what Luke emphasizes in the verse. He reminds us that this experience will happen when the Holy Spirit (Jesus' spirit) comes upon us. The Holy Spirit will be the power to witness. The central idea is that He enables us to be like Him, Jesus, the source of truth. The same Spirit of Jesus would enable the disciples to be the demonstration of the life of Jesus in their world.

This should not surprise us. We know that the theme of the book of Acts (volume 2) and the Gospel according to Luke, (volume 1) is God acting in the world through Jesus, like He does in the Gospel according to Luke, or through the Holy Spirit in the disciples like He does in the book of Acts.

Also the Holy Spirit worked in and through Jesus to produce a demonstration of the Father, in the same way the Spirit of Jesus will work through us to demonstrate the life of Jesus to our world. We are not eyewitnesses of his resurrection or crucifixion, but we are the flesh in which He has come to demonstrate who He is. We are to be his witnesses, a real demonstration of the life of Jesus in this world.

## Not to Do, But To Be

Acts 1:8 says: "you will receive power... and you will be my witnesses..." Could someone who understands the Book of Acts dispute this? Repeatedly, when the power to testify was to be demonstrated, the person was "filled with the Holy Spirit" (Acts 4.8). It is easily seen that the title of the book, "The Acts of the Apostles," doesn't accurately reflect the purpose of the book. The purpose of the book is reflected by the title "The Acts of the Holy Spirit." Were the disciples involved? Yes, they participated, but really they were being the instruments of the Holy Spirit. The book of Acts isn't a story about the disciples and their talents or abilities, but about Jesus and his greatness. He showed himself through people who were filled with Him.

There is a great difference between giving testimony and being a witness. The first is about my actions, while the second is about how I'm being used. One it's about what I proclaim, the other is about what is proclaimed through me. One is about the facts that I say, the other is about the truth that is seen (lived) in my life. One can be explained in terms of training, ability, personality or talent, while the other is about how Jesus is seen in me. One is to talk about Jesus; the other is about Jesus being seen, because he is living through me. One is about the effort; the other it is about relaxing and surrendering. One is about trying to do something and an obligation that we have to fulfill, while the other is about his love, passion and life flowing through me.

In 70 years, the disciples won their whole world for Christ. They didn't achieve it by memorizing phrases or by their good communication techniques. They didn't achieve it by means of their great education, although this is not bad (Acts 4:13). They achieved it through a lifestyle full of God. They were recipients of God's action and they responded to that action. The issue was "to be" not "to do".

Henry Stanley, a reporter, went to spend time in Central Africa with the great missionary, David Livingston. He returned with this report: "If I had been with him longer, I would have been forced to be Christian. By the way, he never talked to me about it".

We have to understand the result of the topic of these two big volumes, the Book of Acts and the Gospel of Luke. Everything is about divine activity. It is about the second person of the Trinity giving up everything he had as God to become a man subject to God. God, through this man Jesus, demonstrated who He was and who He is. It was not about what Jesus was able to do, because constantly he said that He could not accomplish anything by himself. His life was an answer to the action of the Father, by means of the Holy Spirit. The same dynamics took place in the lives of the disciples. They were filled with the Holy Spirit, who was the source of their life. They were witnesses. They were a complete demonstration of Jesus to their world.

# Witness, But Where?

Jesus is very specific in this verse. He said: "in Jerusalem, and in all Judea and Samaria, and to the ends of the earth" (Acts 1:8). If Jesus had only said "to the ends of the earth," the disciples would have focused only on the remote regions and they would have lost sight of their neighbors. If He had only said in Jerusalem, they would have stayed in their Jewish organizational structure and established a sect. But it was clearly a call to demonstrate Jesus' life to the whole world. It included the religious organization that 40 days ago had crucified Jesus. It included the Samaritans, which effectively eliminated any racial barrier demonstration. This means a complete demonstration of the life of Jesus all the time and to all people.

There were no limits to the demonstration of the life Christ through the disciples. Definitively it was fulfilled in the Book of Acts. The disciples demonstrated the life and power of Christ to the lame beggar (Acts 3:6), to the governors, elders and scribes (Acts 4:5). The demonstration of Christ's life also took place through Philip, an Ethiopian (Acts 8:27), to those who persecuted the disciples of the Lord (Acts 2:20). It seems that there is no limit to the demonstrations of Jesus through the lives of the disciples.

## The Divine Activity Through Me

But when you understand the topic of this great book, this is not a surprise. The action of the divine activity is the flow of God into our world through people. When do I have the right to turn off this divine activity? Could it be that if the circumstances turn against me, then I have the perfect excuse for not demonstrating it? What are the attitudes, words or action of another person that force me not to be a witness of Christ? Will skin color or the economic status of a person be a barrier to not allowing Christ to be seen through me? If you can turn off or turn on the demonstration of Christ in your life, then you have enough evidence to know that the demonstration is not His, but yours. Certainly in that case, He is not in control.

I am once again on my knees, in total submission to Him. Ah! So that my life will be a demonstration of his person, because He has come to live through me. Ah! For his demonstration to be consistent, always covering my entire world. This is my prayer.

# The Question That Was Not Asked?

The disciples were excited about the idea that the Kingdom of God would be restored to Israel. They came to Jesus, asking when this would happen. At the time of the crucifixion, they were convinced that the Kingdom of God would never be restored to the sons of Israel. All their hope had vanished. But then, Jesus was raised from the dead and then spent 40 days with them, "and spoke about the Kingdom of God" (Acts 1:3). They pressed Jesus for an answer to their question. They didn't ask once or twice, but repeatedly: "Lord, are you at this time going to restore the kingdom to Israel?" (Acts 1:6).

We have seen the answer from Jesus to his disciples (Acts 1:7-8), but the depth of that answer requires more investigation. This verse (Acts 1:8) is very important for the whole Book of Acts. It is the outline of all that Luke would express in the following pages. This verse is a summary of the message of the book. It is the heart of the "Father's promise" (Acts 1:4).

Luke presents God's activity as the proposition that he wants to emphasize. It is the foundation of the Gospel of Luke and of the Book of Acts. It is the final focus in this passage. Luke states it in such a way that there is no room for adjustments or compromises. There is no way that somebody can reduce the gospel to legalism or simplicity.

## A Spiritual Reality

The idea of Luke is to allow us to see the gigantic change in the disciples, from a physical view of the Spirit of Jesus to a spiritual reality. They moved from doing to being. The self-motivated activity ended and God began flowing through them. The disciples ceased their own efforts, struggles and attempts and they began to relax, learn and depend on God. Luke's emphasis is on the disciples and their total trust in the Spirit of Jesus. The focus is on what the Spirit of Jesus did in them. The actions carried out "in Jerusalem, and in all Judea and Samaria, and to the ends of the earth" (Acts 1:8). The mission was enabled and directed by the Spirit of Jesus. Jesus enabled them to speak appropriately. They spoke clearly in well-known languages. They didn't have to try to be anything - it was impossible for them to form themselves into what they should be. They never again sought positions or glory. The Spirit of Jesus enabled them to "be witnesses" (Acts 1:8). Jesus didn't call the disciples to do anything. They didn't have to be organized. Ecclesiastical structures were not the topic. Numbers, buildings and budgets were not the priority. All the achievements were the result of the Spirit of Jesus. He did miracles, he multiplied the church and he established the witnesses (Acts 2:47).

Clearly we see this in Luke's initial conjunction. Jesus was speaking to the disciples, He was responding to their question. "But..." (Acts 1:8) is a conjunction of distinction that marks a contrast. We have to see verse seven in contrast with verse eight. Jesus was contrasting what the disciples could not know with what they would know and experience then. He said: "It is not for you to know..." (Acts 1:7). The verb "to know" is in the active voice, which means that the subject is responsible for the action of the verb. The subject is related to the disciples who are responsible for the action of knowing. But note that the word "not" makes the phrase negative. The disciples are not responsible for knowing. The "times or dates the Father has set by his own authority" are not under the control of the disciples.

## The Disciples Focus Field

Next Jesus gives them the field for his focus (Acts 1:8). Here was what they would experience! They would succeed through the Spirit of Jesus. What they had been and what they would be would be altered by the Spirit of Jesus. What they had said and would say would be changed by the Spirit of Jesus. What they had done and what they would do would be through the training of the Spirit of Jesus. It was a new day! But you have to understand the key phrase of the verse. Jesus says: "you will receive..." Then he says: "you will be..." But most important are the words contained in the middle of these two truths. Jesus says: "when the Holy Spirit comes on you;" (Acts 1:8). Everything that happens will be of the Spirit of Jesus.

"But you will receive power..." is Jesus' initial phrase. This is a powerful promise given by Jesus. You will receive is a single word in the Greek used in the New Testament. It is a future indicative verb and it means that Jesus is talking about something that will take place. He is just stating a fact. There can be no discussion of this topic. He doesn't try to explain or convince. It is simply the truth! It is something sure!

The same thing applies to the "promise of the Father" (Acts 1:4). The phrase "shall receive power" is an extension of that "promise". The word "promise" communicates the idea that it is given freely. The Father didn't make the promise an obligation. This flowed directly from his heart, which is full of grace. This promise originates in God. He doesn't fulfill his promise because they pressure him, out of obligation or guilt. He gave this promise freely and fulfills it freely. The promise is supported by the loving heart of God. It is certain: "you will receive!"

## There is Power, Matchless Power, in Jesus...

The central point of what you will receive is "power." It is easy for us to misunderstand this central point in the way that the world thinks about power. This world is twisted with selfishness, and that forms the concept of power. From the perspective of the world, power means position, personal gain or self-realization. But Jesus speaks of the opposite concept of the world. The promise of the Father is that we'll receive the Spirit of Jesus, like it is expressed clearly in Acts 1.8: "...when the Holy Spirit comes on you..."

Jesus equates the power to the Spirit of Jesus. In this Spirit there is no selfishness. This power has an attitude of service in the style of the cross. The Spirit of Jesus will enable and enrich our lives, so that all things that we call power are a reflection of God's Spirit. He doesn't give us power, but rather we derive it from his person that lives in us. So each demonstration of the power is a reflection of Him. How can we describe this power? It will be identical to Jesus.

The original Greek word for "power" is the base for the word, dynamite. It is a measurable power because it is demonstrated by means of physical activities. It is explosive in nature and often it changes everything. When it is used in the gospels, it is generally translated as mighty acts. It is an excellent word to describe the movement of Jesus' Spirit through the Book of Acts.

The essence of this word demonstrates the intimacy between the believer and the Spirit of Jesus. The Greek word has to do with the inherent power that resides in something by virtue of its nature. This power doesn't come from something that Jesus' Spirit gives me. It is not like a gun in my hand that gives me the power to rob a bank. The power that you will receive comes from the nature that is inside you. The nature of the Spirit of Jesus which is woven in such a way, with his personality, that you will become what He really designed you to be. It is not something that you have, but rather He has it for you. What you are in Him, really ends up being His power in you. This power demonstrates the Spirit of Jesus living in you.

Paul expressed it in these words: "But we have this treasure in jars of clay to show that this all-surpassing power is from God and not from us" (2 Corinthians 4:7). We cannot learn this in seminars, because it is not the power of knowledge. We don't develop it in training sessions because it is not the result of ability. We don't practice to improve it, because it is not the development of our talents. This is of God. The power resides in the Spirit of Jesus. He shows himself through us. It is like the power and the Spirit of Jesus are the same thing. Just as water and wet are almost synonymous; so are the power and the Spirit of Jesus. One speaks of the other. To think that it is filled with the nature of God and not to demonstrate such power is absurd.

## Full of the Spirit of Christi

Now we come to the parallel phrase: "you will be my witnesses" (Acts 1:8). As in the previous sentence, the verb will be is in the future indicative form. Definitively it speaks of a fact. It is not necessary to defend or to argue a fact, it is simply what it is. Just as "you will receive power", so in the same way it is for sure "you will be my witnesses."

The central point is not about doing, but about being.

The same Greek root that presents the "I Am" from Jesus (John 6:48; 14:6) is used here in reference to us. It has to do with existence, not with performance. It is nature, not activity. It is the fiber and the substance of the person, not their achievements. The emphasis is on who we are, not on what we are doing. This is the "I am" that belongs us!

## To Be Witnesses

What is that "I am"?: "You will be my witnesses" (Acts 1:8). The etymology of the word seems to find its beginnings in the same root of the word that means "to have in mind" or "to be interested". The witness then is somebody who remembers and can talk about something. From the perspective of  Judaism (especially during Christ's time), the meaning of witness was almost always surrounded by suffering. This became true with the use of the word in Christianity. The word "witness" in Greek, is translated into the English word "martyr ".

In Luke's writings, a witness must be combined with the truth. He makes a distinction between fact and truth. To be a witness, one does not simply repeat the facts, but rather he must be possessed by the truth. Start with the apostles and the fact that they had to be eyewitnesses. When the first disciples were replacing Judas Iscariot, they said that the replacement should be "…one of the men who have been with us the whole time that the Lord Jesus went in and out among us, beginning from John's baptism to the time when Jesus was taken up from us. For one of these must become a witness with us of His resurrection." (Acts 1:21-22). To be a witness of Christ's resurrection, the replacement had to have experienced more than just having seen the risen Jesus. He must have been involved with Jesus' teaching, moved by the miracles, desolated by the crucifixion, and to have enjoyed the joy of knowing that Christ lives. This is more than data. This truth that has become passion, involves all that is the person.

The witness to whom Jesus is calling is not who attended the seminar on how to witness and received a certificate. It's the one who has experienced a deep regret for his sin, and has been ashamed of the consequences. He is aware that the cross is the only means of freedom and not a piece of gold on a chain. The witness must cling to the living Christ and find life in Him. He cannot stop testifying because he is a witness.

This is the desire of my heart! This is what I want to receive and what I want to be. When will this happen in my life allowing me to say clearly: "I am a witness"? Perhaps a better question may be: How will this happen to me? Remember the special structure of verse 8 of chapter 1 of Acts. Jesus begins with "you will receive power", and he ends with "you will be my witnesses", but in between these two sentences is the source of that reality, it is the answer to when and how.

## When and How Can I Become a Witness?

Jesus says, "when the Holy Spirit comes on you..." (Acts 1:8). This is his explanation. The answer to the "when?" is in the moment in which the Spirit of Jesus empowers you. This brings us back to focus entirely on the person of Jesus Christ. The fullness of the Holy Spirit in me produces the ties that bind the data with the truth, which brings passion. It is the reality that He is the Truth.

This is the basic topic of Luke's writings in volume one and two. The action of the divine activity is the source of all that is done. The Spirit of Jesus, as we are shown in the Gospel, came to be the Spirit living in the disciples in the Book of Acts. All that happens in and through their lives is a demonstration and training of the Spirit of God.

Did you notice the phrase "comes on"? Jesus emphasizes the idea of "on." The preposition "on" is included in the Greek verb and then "on" is repeated again at the end of the sentence. It is mentioned twice. A literal translation is: "when the Holy Spirit has come upon on you". The complete sentence is call, "genitive absolute" and expresses time, cause or condition. So this phrase, "when the Holy Spirit comes upon you..." is the condition or cause of the previous statement "but you will receive power."

## The Fullness of the Holy Spirit

You will not have power, and you will never be a witness, unless the Holy Spirit has come to produce this within you. Nothing is said to us here about types of personality, talents, experiences or training. Everything is focused on the Spirit of Jesus. Would you conclude that when the Holy Spirit fills you, you cannot avoid being a witness? And that when the Holy Spirit does not fill you, it is impossible to be a witness? Would you conclude that when you are being a witness, the Holy Spirit empowers you and when you are not being a witness, you lack the power of the Holy Spirit? It is impossible to be full of Jesus and not be a witness, and it is impossible to be a witness without being filled with Jesus.

## Total Consecration

In order to fulfill the biblical mandate, first of all, we must get rid of any form of life that is based on ourselves. No other source can be present. There cannot be a mixture of sources; something of Jesus and something of mine. Yes, I will be involved, but I am not the source. Jesus is empowering and expanding our lives so that we "will be my witnesses in Jerusalem, and in all Judea and Samaria, and to the ends of the earth" (Acts 1:8).

# Notes:

# 4 STEPS TO BECOMING A HAPPY TITHER

**Christian Sarmiento**

## Who? Me?

(Knowledge)

This is the first reaction of a person who has just found out, now that they are a Christian, that they should tithe – give ten percent of all of their finances to finance Jesus' mission through the church. So the answer to the question is: Yes, you also need to tithe.

The reason for this answer is that the Bible teaches us clearly that God is the Owner and Lord of everything. We are only stewards or administrators of His creation and of what He gives us to administer.

When we decide to accept Christ as our personal Savior, we are willing to do anything for Him. As a new person in Christ, our thankfulness towards God gives us the energy to testify, pray, and strive to be like our Savior. The Holy Spirit makes it possible for our life to enter a new dimension: A spiritual life.

However, there is the moment when we start to see things from a different perspective. After a few weeks or months, the novelty of being a Christian starts to become routine. We start to reason and question our new life. Sometimes it feels like a large load is about to crush us. Now the feeling of conversion becomes one of voluntary dedication and surrendering. We accept new priorities according to a new scale of values.

As the Holy Spirit guides us, we accept each new value for our new life in Christ. We leave this and that, and our new life is frequently converted into a series of "No's". Our favorite words for our testimony during this phase are: "I don't do... I stopped..."

Then one day, we are taught that tithing is part of this new life. I remember vividly when my pastor read that the Manual of the Church says, "The historical ethical rules of the church are expressed in part in the following: 'The Scriptures teach that God is the Owner of all persons and all things. We, therefore, are His stewards of both life and possessions. God's ownership and our stewardship ought to be acknowledged, for we shall be held personally accountable to God for the exercise of our stewardship. God, as a God of system and order in all of His ways, he has established a system of giving that acknowledges His ownership over all human resources and relationships. To this end all His children should faithfully tithe and present offerings for the support of the gospel.'" (Manual of the Church of the Nazarene)

## Yes, I Tithe!

### (Conviction)

After praying and thinking about tithing, we start questioning the validity of the matter and even the Manual. We start to examine the scriptures and search to see if it is true that God would ask us for an amount, which in the beginning might seem to be a lot: "Tithing!"

We might say to ourselves:

- The church has money. I need it much more than this very big denomination.

- Ten percent of my money is very little for such a big church; it would be better to use that for my own benefit.

- I don't live in the law of the Old Testament, but in the grace of the New Testament.

- After I receive my salary and set aside what I need to live, I don't have any earnings left.

All of these arguments are because we care for our loved ones. The truth is we don't want anyone to hurt or damage our family. When our financial earnings decrease, our family suffers. However, God's spirit is faithful. One day in our devotional reading, we found this:

"'I the LORD do not change. So you, the descendants of Jacob, are not destroyed. Ever since the time of your ancestors, you have turned away from my decrees and have not kept them. Return to me, and I will return to you,' says the LORD Almighty.

But you ask, 'How are we to return?'

'Will a mere mortal rob God? Yet you rob me.'

But you ask, 'How are we robbing you?'

'In tithes and offerings. You are under a curse—your whole nation—because you are robbing me. Bring the whole tithe into the storehouse, that there may be food in my house. Test me in this,' says the LORD Almighty, 'and see if I will not throw open the floodgates of heaven and pour out so much blessing that there will not be room enough to store it.'" (Malachi 3:6-10)

The admonition of the Lord filled us with panic and makes us say, "Let's try it and tithe."

## "Pastor, this is my tithe." ▬▬▬▬

(Obligation)

We start tithing. However, our joy is not complete. Yet we have a smile on our lips as we put our tithe in the offering plate and mentally we say, "Pastor, here is my tithe."

The only biblical reference that the Gospels have recorded from the lips of Jesus as a direct reference to tithing is found in the midst of a series of accusations that He makes to the Scribes and the Pharisees:

"Woe to you, teachers of the law and Pharisees, you hypocrites! You give a tenth of your spices—mint, dill and cumin. But you have neglected the more important matters of the law—justice, mercy and faithfulness. You should have practiced the latter, without neglecting the former." (Matthew 23:23)

The Pharisees came into being around the year 150 B.C.. The Pharisees were not so much a sect, but what we might call a political party, and it had two purposes: First, to assure the exact payment of the tithes and the offerings. Second, to promote the fulfillment of the strictest orders of Levitical purity according to the law.

The Pharisees were excellent tithers and they would turn away from common people that didn't know or care about the oral law. A Pharisee was considered to be an aristocrat, a person that was fussy about religious situations. On the contrary, the average Jew was almost considered a pagan, a publican.

What was Jesus' attitude toward tithes and the payment of offerings?

When Jesus would speak, the multitudes would not only listen attentively, but even in the beginning of His ministry during the Sermon on the Mount, they were amazed by "his doctrine" because he taught as one who had authority and not like the scribes (Matthew 7:28-29). Jesus' enemies were very attentive to each word that he said and each one of his actions. They tried to set traps and accuse him of his slightest fault. Yet they weren't able to accuse him of not paying his tithe. The Scribes and Pharisees asked for his advice frequently and sincerely (John 7:2; Matthew 19:3, 22:36-38; Luke 17:20). As a result they realized that Jesus was well versed in the Scriptures and in Jewish customs.

Based precisely on his knowledge of the Scriptures, Jesus said to his listeners, "Do not think that I have come to abolish the Law or the Prophets; I have not come to abolish them but to fulfill them. For truly I tell you, until heaven and earth disappear, not the smallest letter, not the least stroke of a pen, will by any means disappear from the Law until everything is accomplished. . . For I tell you that unless your righteousness surpasses that of the Pharisees and the teachers of the law, you will certainly not enter the kingdom of heaven." (Matthew 5:17-18,20)

Yes, the Pharisees tithed and were very strict in complying with the law. To this same point, my wife and I arrived – as have many Christians. We give our tithe with a smile on our lips and we think, "Pastor, here is my tithe."

## The Happy Tither

(Happiness)

If our righteousness is greater than that of the Scribes and the Pharisees, then what was Jesus' perspective concerning our obligation to tithe?

Jesus didn't come to abolish the law, but to fulfill it. Tithe is part of that law. In keeping with his mission, when an interpreter of the law asked, "Teacher, what must I do to inherit eternal life?" He responded: "What is written in the law?" (Luke 10:25-26). Jesus referred to the law as the correct standard for conduct of life, which also included tithing. Jesus assumed that his followers have to tithe. Yet he did not stop there. He also presented various principals that we should learn. "Give to the one who asks you, and do not turn away from the one who wants to borrow from you" (Matthew 5:42) He also said, "Give, and it will be given to you. A good measure, pressed down, shaken together and running over, will be poured into your lap. For with the measure you use, it will be measured to you" (Luke 6:38). To his disciples he said, "Freely you have received; freely give." (Matthew 10:8)

Concerning the same issue, our Lord also announced another principal that is unparalleled in world literature. Even though this teaching is not recorded in the Gospels, it apparently made an impression on the minds of the early Christians. The apostle Paul said to the leaders of the church of Ephesus that they should always remember this. "Remembering the words the Lord Jesus himself said, 'It is more blessed to give than to receive'" (Acts 20:35).

Finally, Jesus calls us not only to give part, but to give all, "For where your treasure is, there your heart will be also" (Luke 12:34). When the rich young man came to Jesus saying that he had obeyed the law since his youth (Mark 10:20), Jesus looked at him and loved him. "One thing you lack," he said. "Go, sell everything you have and give to the poor, and you will have treasure in heaven. Then come, follow me." At this the man's face fell. He went away sad, because he had great wealth. Jesus looked around and said to his disciples, "How hard it is for the rich to enter the kingdom of God!"

Yes, tithe. And our righteousness is greater than that of the Pharisees because our wealth, however small it might be (like in the case of the widow's offering in Mark 12:41-44) no longer controls our hearts. We know that if it is necessary, we would abandon everything we have and follow Jesus. We know that it's useless to gain the whole world and lose our souls (see Mark 8:34-38). We give our tithe because we know that it's the least that a grateful heart can do.

In our stewardship, my wife and I have taken these four steps to become happy tithers. The Lord invites us to continue until our righteousness is greater than the Pharisees. Then we will be able to deal with the most important matters of the law: "justice, mercy, and faith" (Matthew 23:23).

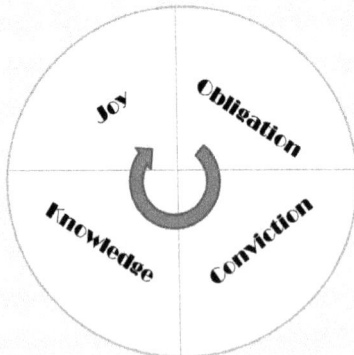

www.ingramcontent.com/pod-product-compliance
Lightning Source LLC
Chambersburg PA
CBHW060926040426
42445CB00011B/810